Britain and European Union

Dialogue of the Deaf

Lord Beloff

First published in Great Britain 1996 by
MACMILLAN PRESS LTD
Houndmills, Basingstoke, Hampshire RG21 6XS
and London
Companies and representatives
throughout the world

A catalogue record for this book is available
from the British Library.

ISBN 0–333–63432–2 hardcover
ISBN 0–333–67192–9 paperback

First published in the United States of America 1996 by
ST. MARTIN'S PRESS, INC.,
Scholarly and Reference Division,
175 Fifth Avenue,
New York, N.Y. 10010

ISBN 0–312–16157–3

Library of Congress Cataloging-in-Publication Data
Beloff, Max Beloff, Baron, 1913–
Britain and European union : dialogue of the deaf / Lord Beloff.
p. cm.
Based on the author's pamphlet: A tale of two Europes.
Includes bibliographical references and index.
ISBN 0–312–16157–3
1. European Union countries—Foreign relations—Great Britain.
2. Great Britain—Foreign relations—European Union countries.
I. Beloff, Max Beloff, Baron, 1913– Tale of two Europes.
II. Title.
D1065.G7B45   1996
327.4104—dc20   96–6786
                                                                   CIP

10   9   8   7   6   5   4   3   2   1
05   04   03   02   01   00   99   98   97   96

Printed and bound in Great Britain by
Antony Rowe Ltd, Chippenham, Wiltshire

Contents

Preface

Although the subject of this short book is one with which I have had an academic concern for half a century it is not itself presented as a piece of original research but as a consideration from available material of the notion of a 'dialogue of the deaf' in this particular context.

I wish to thank Mr T. M. Farmiloe of Macmillan for encouraging me to turn a pamphlet of mine, *A Tale of Two Europes*, into a book.

I have incurred other debts for material and information to: Dr Richard Aldrich, Dr Vernon Bogdanor, Lord Bruce of Donington, Sir Julian Bullard, Dr Anne Deighton, Professor David Dilks, Professor Andrew Durand, Professor Jack Hayward, the Rt Hon. David Howell, MP, Professor Philip James, Lord Jay, Dr Henry Kissinger, Dr Egon Kochanke, Vice-Admiral Louis Le Bailly, Mr Andrew McHallam, Lord Mackenzie Stuart, Sir Patrick Neill, the Hon. Michael Pakenham, David Pannick, QC, the Rt Hon. John Redwood, MP, and Sir Roger Tomkys.

I wish to thank Judith Burns for producing a legible MS out of my tangled original.

All Souls College, Oxford   BELOFF
November 1995

1 The Problem Stated

One feature of international relations, clear in retrospect, is that the participants in policy-making and negotiations often had quite different views of what their interlocutors meant or intended. The basic conceptions of the two sides in confrontation may be so wholly different that no meeting of minds is possible. The first encounters between the inhabitants of the American continent and their Spanish conquerors is an obvious example, given much salience by the outpouring of literature at the time of the Columbus quincentenary in 1992. Another example merely two hundred years ago is the British expedition to China in 1792–4 where the records show that what the British thought their mission had achieved and the way in which the Chinese looked at it were totally at variance with each other.[1] Some might argue that such differences of interpretation of words and symbols still bedevil the relations of the West with China (perhaps also with Japan) in our own day.

The relations of western European countries and the United States with a country itself part of Christendom, Russia, throughout its revolutionary period have also seen a lack of comprehension by the West of what was actually going on there, and a similar inability on the part of Russia's rulers, Tsarist, Communist, or post-Communist, to understand the intentions and motivations of foreign governments.[2]

Yet even within the confines of a single civilisation, similar gaps in mutual comprehension are obviously possible, with dangerous results. One has only to think of the 'appeasement' era in British and French foreign policy in the 1930s to see that its failings were in large measure due to an inability to enter into the mental world of Hitler and the Nazis despite the availability of much evidence as to its content.[3] Sometimes the mental world into which we are called upon to enter in order to frame policy is simply too remote from our own way of thinking for us to be able to

1

grasp it or its possible consequences. Recent debates in the West about the former Yugoslavia or Islamic 'fundamentalism' may be an example.

A survey of past examples of apparent or real incomprehension between different countries shows that the problem is not always what it appears to be on the public record. Statesmen may actually fail to appreciate what others have in mind because of ignorance or lack of imagination. But it is clear that usually they have some warning of what their adversaries intend, and the question is why they ignore such warnings, of which in respect to Nazi Germany there were plenty reaching British statesmen from official and unofficial sources. On occasion one can simply say that it is natural for many people to put the best interpretation that they can on what they perceive. They find it hard to believe in evil – the history of CND would provide useful examples. But it may simply be that they put the less pleasant aspects of what they are told out of their minds because it would necessitate policy decisions which for other reasons they are loath to take. If for financial reasons one wishes to avoid large expenditures on armaments, it is better to diminish one's perception of the threat, so as not to be playing into the hands of political opponents of one's own political party.

Considerations of this kind may lead to a situation in which, while the government itself is fully aware of the threat, the picture it paints for the general public is quite a different one. In other words, there are times in the conduct of foreign policy when the only way to secure backing for what one wants is to tell the electorate less than the truth. And if, as is so often the case, issues of foreign policy are more complicated than those posed by simple aggression or the threat of it, it may well appear to statesmen that it is a positive duty not to let the electorate fully into their confidence.

It is the contention of the present study that Britain's relations with the movement towards creating a European Union or a United States of Europe provide examples both of genuine self-deception and of actual attempts to persuade the British people of things that the persuaders must have known were not true. Since much of the debate is recent and indeed still continuing, one's judgements must be more tentative than when we deal with the more fully documented policies of the interwar period. Yet we know enough for some tentative judgements to be offered.

It is the case that there was in important circles in some continental countries and above all in France and Germany after the Second World War a conviction that their only recourse for avoiding its repetition was the creation of a new organisation of western Europe in which national interests would be sacrificed to the needs of the whole range of participating countries, and that this would involve the subordination of national political processes to supranational institutions charged with giving effect to the degree of integration already achieved, and pushing towards still further integration. In the end – and clearly the timetable has always been a flexible one – the main attributes of sovereignty, that is, the making and interpretation and enforcement of laws, as commercial policy, the issuing of currency and the control of credit, security and defence which had been in modern times the attributes of the nation state, would pass to the new Union, just as in the United States of America these powers are mainly and in some cases wholly within the competence of the federal government. Arkansas may have an input into Washington but it cannot declare war, raise armies, issue currency, enact commercial tariffs, decide upon the basic rate of interest or legislate effectively in ways ruled by the Supreme Court to be contrary to the Constitution of the United States.

This view of the future has its adherents in Britain and some of them have never disguised the fact. But they have always been a minority. What has been the common position of most British statesmen throughout the fifty years under consideration has been their hope for a different kind of Europe, in which the eradication of the old causes of armed conflict and the pursuit of common economic and social goals would ultimately rest upon the actions of nation states, using the supranational organisations as vehicles for their common purposes when this seemed desirable. This alternative vision was and is held to offer two advantages – the ability of countries to retain the distinctiveness of their own institutions and ways of life, and the ability to extend their common working to countries which at the time when the concept of European union was launched seemed to be totally enveloped in the Soviet grip. The story is thus one of two alternative 'Europes'.[4]

Statesmen who have represented this majority view have sometimes taken it as proved that this made membership of the European Communities, now embraced within the European Union, impossible, and led to overt opposition to British membership at the crucial moments under governments of both major political parties. But others have managed to persuade themselves that the two views of Europe were compatible, indeed that membership of the Communities and latterly of the Union was the best way of achieving the British objective. For much of the period the European issue was subordinated to other considerations, in particular the maintenance of concord within the major parties.

To some extent the British position was inevitably determined by the attitudes of continental governments. Some adhered to the belief that British objectives were indeed incompatible with the kind of united Europe they were trying to create, such as the interpretation placed upon the British position by General de Gaulle when as President of France in 1963 he exercised his veto against British entry.[5] Others took the view that once admitted into the Communities, the force of circumstances would bring Britain into line and that any concessions to Britain's immediate demands in the form of special provisions or derogations would prove only temporary.

While those continental statesmen keenest for their own reasons on admitting Britain or later on keeping her in tended to play down the pressures on Britain to conform, there were always those, particularly in the Commission, who made no secret of their desire for total integration and their reluctance to concede a special position for any member country except for a short transitional period. The temptation for British leaders who believed that membership was the right way to achieve Britain's own desires was therefore to play down the divergences between continental statesmen and themselves and to give their own interpretation of the Communities or the Union as though it were generally acceptable to their partners. The question that has to be asked is how far British statesmen in making this case genuinely deluded themselves, or were prepared to be less than honest with the electorate so as to secure its backing for their policies.

While the referendum of 1975 is often held to have demonstrated the appeal of the idea of participation in the construction of 'Europe', it would be hard to see then or at any other time a strongly felt desire in Britain to accept the kind of constitutional and political sacrifices that would be entailed. The main support for membership has come from those who saw the possibility of economic benefits from remaining in or the economic dangers that would result from being left out or latterly from trade unionists and socialists who thought that 'Europe' could be invoked to counterbalance the market philosophy of post-1979 British governments. Two sections of the elite, and their adherents in academe and the media, thus came together to persuade the British people that they knew what was good for the country and that those who disagreed did so out of an unworthy nostalgia.

It is not that this aspect of the story is unique to the United Kingdom. To persuade peoples to surrender their sovereignty is always difficult. The history of the making and ratification of the Constitution of the United States even when the states themselves had enjoyed so short a period of self-government shows how hard this can be. And the difficulty was obviously bound to be greater when one was dealing with nation states many of which had had a history of independence for centuries. The technique of persuasion in such circumstances is bound to be similar. The first thing is to state objectives so self-evidently desirable that hardly anyone could be found to repudiate them. In postwar Europe the need to avoid a recurrence of its internecine conflicts was generally conceded. Less obvious but widely accepted was the idea that some of the origins of the recent conflicts had been in the economic policies of the nation states concerned – beggar-my-neighbour forms of protectionism. So the freeing of trade in the broadest sense was seen as a powerful instrument for avoiding a recurrence of past follies.

What next had to be done by those who wished to achieve these ends by the supranational or federal route was to persuade the voters that this route was the only one by which these desirable objectives could be reached. To this effort however had to be added arguments addressed to the interests of the particular nation whose support was being sought. These interests might be easily reconcilable or they might be in contradiction with each other.

At the beginning of the European enterprise, the French had to be made to see it as their guarantee against a future German hegemony – the Communities were to be a way of keeping Germany under control. For the Germans on the contrary – occupied and ostracised – it was their way back to autonomy and respectability. For Italy, recovering from Fascism and defeat, much the same argument applied. Similar political considerations explain the enthusiasm of post-Franco Spain to enter the club. The Benelux countries, part of the original Six, had in recent times been victims rather than makers of history and had everything to gain if the hopes placed in the Communities were to prove correct. Yet even here the appeal had to be different ones where the Netherlands and Belgium were separately concerned. It was not therefore to be wondered at that the protagonists of Union in every country should try out arguments derived from possible conceptions of the national interest and that some should be persuaded that they were correct.

It has been common in recent years for those in favour of Britain's membership to argue that such difficulties as Britain has had to face have been the consequence solely of its failure to enter the Communities at the time of their creation. We are told that a historic opportunity was missed. But such arguments overlook the extent to which the whole enterprise was an essentially Franco-German one, as indeed it has largely remained.

The 'Common Market' of the Treaty of Rome was based upon a precise bargain – a Common Agricultural Policy would shore up the French peasant class, the basis of successive French regimes, and also ease its decline, and at the same time the markets of France and the other original members would be thrown open to German industry and enable it to rebuild after its diversion into war preparations under the Nazis and the tackling of large-scale physical destruction created by the war. Much has changed in the European economy since the early days, and more is changing as the upheaval in the East and the impact of German reunification make themselves felt.

Defence issues, always a neuralgic spot, have taken on a new aspect with the end of the 'Cold War' and the shift in the priorities of the United States. Many devices have had to be found to satisfy the needs of the original members and the later adherents to the system. But at every crisis the original Franco-German core re-emerges. It is difficult to see how British membership from the beginning could have altered or would have been allowed to alter the original contract on which the whole system has rested.

What we do not know is how far the experience of the Communities (now the Union) has become so much part of the daily round and ordinary thinking of the peoples of the member states in general for the survival of the system to be taken for granted and its professed goals of a more complete integration plausible. Within seventy years of the coming into effect of the American Constitution, the United States witnessed a devastating civil war. Less than a hundred and fifty years after the passage of the British North America Act and the coming into being of the Dominion of Canada, powerful elements in francophone Canada still urge the desirability of a separate Quebec. Nor is it only in federal states that we see centrifugal tendencies gaining ground. To investigate the current appeal of the Union in continental Europe would be beyond the capacities of the present writer. What is intended in the present study is to see what lessons can be derived from the British engagement with the idea of European union, and how to explain the persistent peculiarities of the British approach.

For the latter part of this task, what has been said already about the nature of the Communities is highly pertinent. Their establishment and growth involved the creation of a new interlocutor on the international scene composed of the members of the Commission and their staffs. Foreign offices geared to dealing with other sovereign governments were bound to take some time to get used to this novelty. It is true that in a very general fashion, all international (as opposed to supranational) institutions acquire some kind of corporate personality often embodied in the person of their Secretary-General. But while one may talk of opinion at the United Nations meaning what the Secretary-General and his adjuncts believe at a given time, in the last resort it will be governments acting through the Security Council or occasionally the General Assembly who decide what shall be done. And the same is true of the Secretary-General of even so close-knit an alliance as NATO. Like the permanent secretaries of domestic government departments, even these high functionaries are civil servants. But the members of the European Commission do not see themselves as civil servants but as independent voices on the international scene. And where they have a collective point of view, expressed by the President of the Commission, he has increasingly demanded to be treated in international gatherings as another head of state, even though the state in question does not yet exist.[6]

In framing relations with the Community the British government has had to deal with this unique institution. But it has also had to deal with the other member states each of whom, as already made clear, will have its own list of national goals and priorities. Indeed in some cases – the Greeks are the outstanding example – they have little or no concern with general issues of policy but simply see the whole organisation as a way of channelling funds to themselves from the taxpayers of wealthier nations. This is not to say that relations with some of the smaller countries are unimportant. Particularly with the advent of majority voting their support on some issues can be essential. But if one thinks of the period as a whole, it is obvious that the key question has been Britain's relations with the two pillars of the system – France and Germany. And here again there is some reason to believe that there have been failures in perception. So one has to go back to the beginning.

Before approaching matters of substance it may be as well to get out of the way the question of nomenclature, since it may be the case that the establishing of attitudes in Britain has been made more difficult by confusion as to the proper names of the entities to which it has been held we should, or should not, adhere. I do not here refer to the major issues of principle surrounding such concepts as 'supranational' and 'federal' which will be discussed in a subsequent chapter. It is a question of how to refer to particular bodies at particular times. The confusion has arisen because of the complicated history of their establishment.

The Coal and Steel Community (ECSC) was set up in 1950. In 1957, the six member countries established two new 'communities', the European Economic Community (EEC) and the European Atomic Energy Community (Euratom), by two Treaties of Rome which entered into effect in 1958. From the beginning the basic institutions of all three Communities – the Commission, the Council and the Assembly – were the same. And in 1967 the three communities were formally merged, though in law they continued to exist. In June 1979, the first direct elections were held for the Assembly which in 1987 formally adopted the title of Parliament, though this had been used in practice for some time already.

In somewhat similar fashion the European Economic Community began to refer to itself as the European Community and this usage was made formal by the Treaty of Maastricht in 1991 whereby what had been the EEC became the EC.

The Maastricht Treaty which came into force in 1993 created the European Union consisting of the Communities and the arrangements for the two intergovernmental 'pillars' dealing with home affairs and foreign policy and security matters in which the Community institutions of the Commission and Court have no role.

A further difficulty is that while 'European Union' is the name of the whole structure created by the Treaty of Maastricht it was also used throughout the period as a phrase for the more general goal of the entire process of 'European integration' by which has been meant the transfer of functions, hitherto the prerogative of sovereign states, to joint institutions.

Since what follows is not a legal textbook but an essay, I have used whichever terms seem least cumbersome, which in general means using the term 'European Community' for most of the pre-Maastricht period as well as for that part of the Maastricht structure which it embodies. The same is true of the use of 'Assembly' and 'Parliament'.

Except from lawyers one must not expect precision in political debate which is the proper subject of this book but one does need to keep in mind that among the electorate there was throughout considerable confusion as to who was responsible for what. Even after the lapse of time since Britain adhered to the European Convention on Human Rights and entered the Communities, one is always coming across references that suggest that there is confusion between the Court at Strasbourg and the Court at Luxembourg. But since one also comes across examples of confusion between the House of Lords in its legislative capacity and the House of Lords in its judicial capacity, it is perhaps not just foreign institutions which are only vaguely perceived by those who have no compelling reason to understand them. It may be that such confusion made it easier for protagonists of 'European unity' to get their way with consequences that were by 1995 only just beginning to be realised as the European Union moved into the crisis which is the subject of the concluding chapter.

2 The Historical Perspective

Relations between the inhabitants of Britain and their continental neighbours precede the Roman conquest – the first event in Britain's history of which we have detailed knowledge. Since that event those relations have been central to its existence whether on the political, the cultural or the economic plane. Yet their development has never been a straightforward affair. It is significant that a recent effort to tell the whole story should have been published under the title *Convergence or Divergence?*.[1] The question is then whether the latest phase, signalised by Britain's adherence to the European Communities and now the European Union marks yet another case of convergence or whether it represents a final irrevocable choice. Are the marks of distinctiveness which have shown themselves from time to time now in process of being abandoned to the extent that over large areas of activity the British will be seen as partners in some pan-European enterprise?

One might ask indeed whether such an outcome might not bring a final resolution to some of the problems arising within the British Isles themselves in the course of the past two millennia. Can the Anglo-Irish conflict endemic in one form or another since the Norman period be resolved by virtue of the fact that both Britain and Ireland are members of the wider grouping? Or, on the contrary, can bonds that have been forged between England and Scotland now safely be relaxed, and Scotland become a separate nation state within the European Union as the outcome of its quite different experience of 'convergence and divergence'? And what of Wales?[2] It is curious in this context to reflect that Wales has seen some success for the linguistic nationalism also alive in parts of the continent while in Ireland, despite efforts to revive and safeguard the language, it is not the principal component of its modern self-image. Or again

11

what significance can be attached to the fact that Ireland shares with England, most of the United States and most of the Commonwealth an attachment to the common law, while Scotland's legal heritage, like that of the rest of western Europe, is essentially that of Roman law? For the moment we can ignore these questions, important though they are, since the membership of the European Union is that of the United Kingdom accepted by the Westminster Parliament in which England, Scotland, Wales and Northern Ireland are represented, but the Irish Republic is not. And in that Parliament the balance of population means that the decisive voice is that of England. So it is upon England rather than 'Britain' that we need to concentrate our attention.

When Hugh Gaitskell declared that for Britain to enter a European Federation would mean becoming 'no more than a "Texas" or "California" in the United States of Europe' and that what Britain would be throwing away in order to become a 'province of Europe' would be a 'thousand years of history',[3] it was English history that he must have had in mind. Britain was not politically a concept with a thousand years behind it. In this respect Gaitskell was sharing in Winston Churchill's vision of the uniqueness of England's experience as well as that of her interests. Churchill had always made it plain that while he welcomed the contribution to peace which some kind of structure embodying the countries on the two sides of the Rhine might make, Britain could not be part of it.[4] Even so, a 'thousand years of history' must be regarded as a rhetorical exaggeration in respect of political sovereignty in the modern sense. During the period after the withdrawal of Roman power, when England was largely repeopled by Angles and Saxons from northern Europe, the rivalries between their rulers and their battles against the retreating Britons were carried on in a country whose links with continental Europe were only religious and cultural. But later on, England became part of a short-lived Danish empire and after an interlude of native English rule part of a Norman, and later Angevin, empire. England was immersed in the politics of its neighbours and through participation in the crusades even of those further afield. Not until the end of the Hundred Years War and the abandonment of possessions on the European mainland can we see the emergence of the modern English nation state. Five hundred years of history would be nearer the mark.

The sixteenth century is in many respects the turning-point. Not only did the English Crown cease to have continental possessions to worry about – the position was temporarily altered by the link under the Hanoverian kings with their German electorate – but also carried through after many vicissitudes a church settlement which was subordinate to the secular authority and tended to align England (and after the Union, Scotland as well) with the Protestant cause in Europe. It is fair to add that this break followed a long period in which the powers of the Pope had been challenged, particularly where money was concerned. John Wycliffe's affirmative reply to the query from Richard II's Great Council as to whether England could keep for her own defence money which the Pope wished to transfer abroad from the Church in England shows that as early as 1377 the issue was a live one; nor is it irrelevant to quote his remarks that what claim the Pope had must be for alms and that 'charity begins at home and it would be not a work of charity but of fatuity to send the alms of the realm to foreigners'. The King's letter to the Archbishop of Canterbury dated 10 October 1389 and the subsequent statutes of Provisors (1390) and Premunire (1393) may have had distant echoes in our time in the minds of those confronted with pecuniary demands not from the Pope of Rome but under the Treaty of Rome.[5]

The centuries between the Norman Conquest and the coming to the throne of the Tudors also saw the groundwork for two aspects of the British scene which point to divergence rather than convergence. The first, already referred to, was in respect of the legal system. The English common law was the work of the courts of the Norman and Plantagenet kings deciding cases on the basis of existing Saxon codes and practices. The courts themselves carried on their business in Norman French, the language of the upper classes, until gradually it was superseded by English, an amalgam of the languages of the conquerors and the conquered. In 1362 ancient custom bowed to the change and it was decreed that henceforth pleadings should be in English, not 'French', though they would still be enrolled in Latin.[6] The common law was seen by later generations to be a guarantee of the rights of Englishmen and superior to the Roman law which was held to justify absolutism.

The other main development in the Middle Ages which the Tudors managed to incorporate in their approach to the government of the country was Parliament. Assemblies of estates were not unknown in continental countries but in the course of the sixteenth and seventeenth centuries their monarchs found means of dispensing with them. Only in England was the legislative power, that is to say, the capacity for making statutes to fill gaps in the common law or clarify its provisions, to become and remain a matter for the King in Parliament. Parliament also acquired the power of the purse. By the eighteenth century British national sentiment could feed easily upon the idea of Protestantism and parliamentary government being set in permanent opposition to Roman Catholicism and monarchical absolutism. The fit was not perfect but the images were powerful.

Historians of a sociological bent would see the development of both the common law and parliamentary institutions as evidence of a substantial difference between the course of economic and social development in England and that of most of Europe, with an earlier acceptance of private property and its protection as the norm, and serfdom and other forms of dependence as vanishing or declining factors while still vigorous on the continent.[7] By the sixteenth century it was clear to Englishmen themselves and to foreigners that they were different from other Europeans and happy in the difference. No other European nation had as potent a symbol for national pride as the defeat of the Spanish Armada. Its literary reverberations were to continue into the nineteenth century.

From the point of view of Britain's relations with continental countries, it does not matter too much whether we take the traditional Whig view that the modern British state began with the Glorious Revolution of 1688–9 and the Union with Scotland in 1707 or whether we take the view that some kind of *ancien régime* persisted until the major reforms of the 1830s.[8] What matters is that in Britain and in Britain alone there was an unbroken constitutional development so that such new factors as universal suffrage and the dependence of the executive upon the confidence of the legislature were incorporated into existing structures. There was no clearing away of ancient institutions and the setting up of wholly new ones as in the outcome of the French Revolution and the Napoleonic conquests. Nor did Britain have to face the upheavals which affected all of central and eastern Europe as a result of the First World War. Finally, while another wave of destruction overwhelmed most of continental Europe as a result of the Nazi conquests so that once again in 1945 many countries had to fashion their political systems anew, the continuity of British constitutional practice remained unimpaired.

Other contrasts are no harder to draw. Elizabeth I was not only the first monarch since the Norman Conquest to rule no possessions on continental European soil but also the monarch to whose reign one looks for the beginnings of British expansion overseas. The major part of the first British Empire in North America which had begun under her successor ended with the successful revolt of the American colonies culminating in the Treaty of Paris of 1783. But by then the foundations had been laid for the second British Empire which at the time of its greatest extent in 1921 covered a large part of the globe. The difference that this made was already clear in the eighteenth century. While the rulers of the European states fought each other or negotiated over territorial claims at each other's expense, Britain, dominant on the seas, was primarily concerned not to see that dominance overthrown.[9]

Other countries also acquired overseas possessions in the Americas, where Spain had preceded Britain, and later on in Africa and the archipelagos of the Indian Ocean. In the period after 1945 these empires were, like Britain's

liquidated but here again the experience would be a different one and figure differently in the arguments over
'Europe'. Meanwhile the development of self-governing institutions, first in the countries of white settlement – the
Old Dominions – and latterly in the Indian Empire and the
colonies helped to instil in British opinion still further
admiration for their own parliamentary system, while the
acceptance of the Privy Council as a common court of last
resort for Britain's overseas possessions helped in the further
dissemination of the common law.

Once again historians of a different bent might look at the
same developments in different ways. It could be said that
the spread of imperial rule or influence was dictated by the
way in which Britain's own economic policy was shaped –
looking for the widest possible area in which to find markets
or seek for food and raw materials, in contrast to the strong
continental preference for more self-contained economic
systems upheld by protectionism.[10]

Both the economic argument and the emphasis on the
need to preserve the Commonwealth (into which by now the
Empire had been transformed) figured more prominently
than the controversies over the role of Parliament or the
future of the legal system in the debate over entry into the
European Communities in the 1960s and early 1970s and in
the referendum campaign on the issue in 1975. And even
though experience with the operations of the Brussels institutions and the European Court gave the constitutional
question greater salience in the negotiation and ratification
of the Treaty of Maastricht in 1991–3, it was still given less
prominence than the economic aspect of what was being
done.

It remains to account for the apparent connivance of so
many people who should have been the upholders of the
traditional position with the successive inroads that were
being made upon it. On the whole it was obviously Parliament rather than the law itself which was most widely seen
as in danger of being downgraded. It is true that in recent
years the emphasis formerly given to British constitutional
history in the educational system and in the training of the

British elites has declined. But in so far as there is even a modicum of understanding of Britain's past it is closely linked with the role of Parliament. Schoolchildren in their thousands come to the Palace of Westminster and see in the nineteenth century murals some of the great events in its history – Speaker Lenthall and the Five Members, for instance. Television has made people aware of Parliament's connection with the monarchy through the annual ceremony of the State Opening. Most people assume that the House of Commons remains the central feature of our public life, and their own MP their natural recourse if they have a grievance in relation to governmental activity. Even though there has been some decline in voter participation, it remains high and is in sharp contrast to the lack of interest in the elections to the European Parliament which has never been taken seriously in this country. Had Parliament shown itself alive to the extent to which it was handing over its principal functions established over centuries to the new European institutions and defied the wishes of successive governments by refusing to do so, it could certainly have relied on massive popular understanding and support, as would not have been true in most continental countries where parliamentary institutions are more novel and more fragile.

The question is clearly political rather than legal. By passing the European Communities Act and the Single European Act and ratifying the Maastricht Treaty, Parliament divested itself of powers in a way which conforms to what Dicey held to be one of the two pillars of the constitution – parliamentary sovereignty.[11] Whether members of Parliament fully understood what they were doing and whether if they had understood it other considerations would have been set aside needs further inquiry. What is indubitable is that Dicey's other basic principle, the rule of law, has been set aside, in the sense that what Dicey meant was the rule of the common law of England composed of both the decisions of the English courts and parliamentary statutes.

The puzzle that confronts one here is not so much why ministers, civil servants and members of Parliament should have behaved as they did but why the English legal profession and its leaders in the judiciary should have been so oblivious as to what was going on and so willing to see their role diminished. Most established interests fight for what they regard as their rights: the peers in the period leading up to the Parliament Act of 1911, trade union leaders in respect of the legislation of the Heath and Thatcher governments, the organised medical profession at various junctures. Not so the judges.

Various possibilities suggest themselves. In the first place, there is the argument that making law is a matter for Parliament and negotiating treaties a matter for the Executive – judges simply decide cases as they arise. Such an attitude would no doubt fortify their inclination towards prudence but may not suffice to explain everything.

The second possible explanation is that members of the British legal profession including the judges were already familiar with the extent to which conventions entered into under international law could have domestic applications which they found acceptable. They thus underrated the extent to which the Communities embodied a new method of legislation and adjudication which had no precedent and was far more of a challenge to Britain's legal system. In particular there was general acceptance of the European Convention on Human Rights and the Commission and Court at Strasbourg responsible for dealing with cases arising under it, both the work of an international, not supranational, institution, the Council of Europe. One piece of evidence in favour of this hypothesis is provided by a major figure in the English legal world, Lord Hailsham, twice Lord Chancellor. In his book *On The Constitution*, published in 1992, he refers to the Convention and to his belief (shared by other eminent lawyers) that it would simplify matters if it were incorporated into English law. And when he goes on to the membership of the Community he admits that though it had been foreshadowed by the machinery of the Convention it does 'juristically speaking' involve a more revolutionary change since 'the rule of the direct application in our domestic law does involve a prac-

tical limitation on the sovereign powers of Parliament'. To
that he appears reconciled without entering into the question as to what the 'Constitution' now means. He cannot
visualise withdrawal from the Community and once again
echoes the political commonplace that British membership
should conduce to its being outward-looking. But when he
comes to describe the machinery of the Community – this
was written pre-Maastricht – he avoids a constitutional
analysis of its powers, treating the Council of Ministers as
an 'Executive' rather than as a legislature and objecting to
the refusal of the Commission, or, as he styles it, a 'Euro-
cracy', to accept the status of civil servants. To Lord
Hailsham, Dicey's principles remain valid though under
pressure (from internal as well as external developments).
And where one might have expected some account of the
input of the European Court of Justice – a far more important
body than the Strasbourg Court – we do not get it.[12]

A third reason for the acquiescence of the judiciary may
derive from the very longevity of the common law system
itself. Its practitioners had managed so far to live with any
number of changes in the economy, in the social structure
and in popular attitudes that they could see no reason to
believe that the system could not survive some new injection
of however unfamiliar a kind. Just as members of Parliament
retained the illusion that they were still possessed of sovereign law-making power, so lawyers continued to believe that
English courts would still fulfil their traditional role. Why
should benchers of the Inns of Court following their comfortable rituals worry about what a gaggle of foreign jurists
were doing at Luxembourg, particularly when English lawyers who did become members of the Court did not sound
the alarm.

The fourth reason may lie in a general misunderstanding
of the differences between English law, particularly English
statute law, and the legislation coming from the Community
and based on continental models. English statute law deals
in detail with what is allowed and what is prohibited,
seeking to provide for most foreseeable eventualities. In
other legal systems it is possible to proceed by enacting

broad principles and leave it to the judges to interpret the enactments by reference to other broad principles. In the case of 'European' legislation two consequences have followed. In the first place, it has been thought necessary in Britain in framing secondary legislation in pursuit of Community directives to cover the ground in as much detail as possible, leaving little doubt as to the duties imposed upon the citizens or businesses involved. In the second place it has meant a persistent misunderstanding of the role of the European Court of Justice by a false analogy with the House of Lords in its appellate capacity. The House of Lords seeks to fathom the intentions of the legislation and to see what the impact would be on a particular case while where possible preserving the authority of precedent. The European Court has as a guiding principle its role in forwarding the policy of ever closer union present in the Treaty of Rome.

Britain's legal heritage does not include a written constitution. But the Treaty of Rome as subsequently amended is for the European Court of Justice precisely that – a constitution, even if an imperfect one, by which it is bound. It is not that British lawyers have no experience of handling written constitutions – the Privy Council in handling appeals from Commonwealth countries has often had to do it – but that the parallel has not been visible.

The most useful lesson would have been that derived from a study of the American Supreme Court and the way in which in the early years of the Republic it furthered the development of the Constitution along particular lines. Indeed for most of its history it has not been a neutral tribunal. The failing would seem to lie in the fact that though much is made of the relationship between the British and American legal systems – the American Bar Association periodically holds its annual convention in London and appropriate speeches are made – English lawyers have not been inclined to make a link between what they know of the United States and what has recently been happening in Europe.

All this is more than a matter of legal theory. One aspect of the British legal tradition is that British subjects regard themselves as bound to observe the law in all its detail. And this attitude has been equally true of that growing portion of the law which emanates directly or indirectly from Brussels. Britain has one of the highest records of compliance with European law among member states. Others procrastinate about putting through measures to implement directives, and fail to provide themselves with the machinery necessary to monitor implementation. It also means that when some particular irritation emerges, Britain will not seek to find a way of managing the situation so as to minimise this effect. 'To British civil servants,' it has been written, 'regardless of ideological sympathies, the law is the law, is the law. To apply it selectively is to tread the path to despotism. To European Community officials this is "a very very British attitude". To them compromise and the sensible application of the blind eye are preferable to a rigid legalism'.[13]

It would seem that Britain's belief that it is above all the country of pragmatism and that it is only foreigners who are motivated by ideology does not hold good in the important area of law. Britain's inheritance from its past does not exclude certain commitments to principle; it is just that they are not the same as other people's. In no area is the dialogue of the deaf more apparent or more dangerous than in this fundamental matter of law, though the dispute about federalism to which we shall have to turn later runs it close.

While the British judiciary has contributed to the failure to apprehend the nature of the changes involved in adherence to the Treaty of Rome and its later amendments, the impetus to joining the Community came from the political and civil service establishment with support from particular sections of the business world. Although the political leaders of Britain in the immediate postwar years no doubt shared in some of the attitudes resulting from an appreciation of Britain's historical experience over the centuries, their own immediate reaction to the dilemmas of policy-making were mainly the result of their own understanding of the lessons to be drawn from the events they themselves had witnessed during their adult lives – the First

World War, the interwar period and above all the 'appeasement' years, and the Second World War from which the
country had just emerged.[14]

Awareness of Britain's economic weaknesses was not
altogether balanced by the recollection of the hour when
Britain 'stood alone'. In that hour all Britain could call upon
were the resources of the Commonwealth and Empire and
the extent to which these resources had been made available
helped to diminish the awareness of the degree to which the
interwar years had seen a loosening of the imperial bonds
and a movement away from rather than towards greater
decision-making at the centre.[15] From the trading and above
all the financial point of view, the advantages of maintaining
the Commonwealth in some form were bound to bulk large
and the dangers to those links were prominent in the
thinking of those who formed the core of the original
opposition to Britain's attempt to enter the Communities.
What was overlooked was that maintaining the Commonwealth links and the responsibilities for defence which this
effort implied was a net drain on Britain's domestic resources which successive governments would find themselves
unable to afford. From the abandonment of the Indian
Empire by the Attlee Labour government, through the
failure to create a viable British sphere of control in the
Middle East, signalised by the 'Suez' débâcle under Anthony Eden, to Harold Macmillan's 'wind of change' speech
with its heralding of the end of British empire in Africa –
Britain's external relations were dominated by this great
retreat. It is not a coincidence that the author of the 'wind
of change' speech should also have been the Prime Minister
who first applied for Community membership.

The second lesson drawn from wartime and interwar
experience was that the key to Britain's security lay with the
United States and would remain there even in the new
'nuclear' world. However one looked at it there was no
escaping the fact that only American military might had
twice prevented the installation of a permanent German
domination of Europe. And the same was true of the defeat
of Japan's attempt to become the dominant power in most

of Asia. It was also clear that it was the infusion of American aid that had helped to prevent the Bolshevik Revolution from attaining its further aims in the darkness and confusion of central and eastern Europe that followed the collapse of the Hohenzollern and Habsburg empires. Only the United States could prevent Stalin and the Red Army breaking through the lines laid down at Yalta and Potsdam and bringing the limits of Soviet rule from the Elbe to the Channel, the Mediterranean and the Atlantic.[16]

Attempts by elements on the British Left to explore the possibility of an alternative scenario of cooperation with the Soviet Union were doomed to frustration by the total unwillingness of Stalin to make any concessions to the principle of national self-determination in the area under Red Army control. Anti-American rumblings continued for a long time on the Left and among sections of the British intelligentsia, though few went as far as their French counterparts. Alignment and practical cooperation with the United States remained at the forefront of the ambitions of successive governments of both British parties and the inception of the Marshall Plan and its embodiment in the Organisation for European Economic Co-operation (OEEC) a continuing point of reference.

There were two obstacles to an even greater measure of Anglo-American joint action in the postwar world. In the first place there was the continued American rejection of what the United States saw as British imperialism or colonialism – a source of difficulty even between Roosevelt and Churchill which was even more to the fore at the time of 'Suez'.[17]

The second obstacle more directly relevant to our present theme was the result of the early American enthusiasm for the idea of a 'United States of Europe' as a means of avoiding the European wars in which the United States had to its regret twice become involved. While in the early stages of the process of integration in Europe, there had been doubts expressed as to the impact of such a development upon world trade in general and the exports of the United States in particular, the political arguments had proved

decisive.[18] This conclusion was obvious to someone working
in Washington in the latter part of 1961:

> By the summer of 1961 there was in the relevant sectors
> of the United States administration a fairly clear doctrine
> regarding the American position on the question of
> European unity. The doubts of the multilateralist econo-
> mists had been put on one side and there was a strong
> commitment to the view that the creation of a United
> States of Europe should take precedence over all other
> considerations.[19]

It was further clear by that stage that the 'European
communities should be expanded to include Britain and the
two Scandinavian members of NATO'.

The view that Britain should find its destiny within a
united western Europe rather than in some particular relationship with the United States was not unconnected with
the American welcome to the winding-up of the British
Empire and American suspicion largely on economic
grounds of the surviving Commonwealth links. The link
became explicit in the speech delivered on 5 December
1962 by Dean Acheson, one of the leading figures in the
Truman Administration and a principal progenitor of the
OEEC and NATO.[20] 'Britain', he told his student audience,

> has lost an empire and not yet found a role. The attempt
> to play a separate power role – that is a role apart from
> Europe, a role based on a 'special relationship' with the
> United States, a role based on being the head of a
> 'commonwealth' which has no political structure, or
> unity, or strength, and enjoys a fragile and precarious
> economic relationship by means of the sterling area and
> preferences in the British market – this role is about
> played out.[21]

Acheson's public intervention was no departure from his
current more private activity in seeking to influence President Kennedy in favour of a new concept of American
foreign policy based upon the idea of an Atlantic partnership with two partners only – the United States and a

United Europe. Acheson was deeply influenced in putting forward such ideas by Jean Monnet who, having got the Communities established, had now turned his attention to the wider sphere.[22] In March 1961 and again in April 1962, Monnet was engaged in talks with Acheson at Washington and was brought by him in touch with other members of the Kennedy circle.[23]

In defending Acheson against the British outcry about his speech the State Department in a public statement on 7 December 1962 pointed out that the general thrust of Acheson's remarks was in line with official State Department policy – 'support for British entry into the European Economic Community, increased economic co-operation by all western nations, and a build-up of conventional military power in Europe'.[24] British indignation was however less concentrated upon the reference to Britain's role in Europe than to Acheson's general downplaying both of Britain's position in the world and the reality of the Commonwealth link. Indeed in his published reply – itself a possibly unique occasion of a British Prime Minister formally replying to a private citizen of another country – Harold Macmillan said that he feared that Acheson's denigration of Britain's world status would add to the difficulties of obtaining British membership of the EEC.[25]

Acheson was not unique among American statesmen in seeking to bring pressure to bear on Britain to accept membership of a European union and to overlook the many differences – other than Commonwealth ties – that made such membership hard to reconcile with Britain's national interest or self-image. Such attitudes were not confined to the Democratic Party but extended to the Republicans. Henry Kissinger, the most reflective of Republican policy-makers, did have the advantage of understanding the degree to which among the European countries themselves, it was considerations of national interest that decided their attitude towards European integration. In retrospect he emphasises 'Suez' as the turning-point. After the enforced climb-down by Britain and France, Adenauer said to de Gaulle: 'Europe will be your revenge.' France did indeed seek a *rapprochement*

with Germany which would take a European shape in the
Treaty of Rome in 1957 and eventually in the de Gaulle–
Adenauer treaty of friendship and consultation in January
1963. Britain, in Kissinger's view, derived from Suez the
opposite lesson, seeking a closer association with the United
States in the hope of influencing US policy.[26] On the French
side, de Gaulle's reaction to the 1959 Berlin crisis was that
'France would concede German military and economic
power, even its pre-eminence in these fields, and would
support German unification in exchange for Bonn's recognition of France as the *political* leader of Europe'.[27] At the
same time, a report from a US intelligence agenda forecast
that if a 'US–UK combination appears to be moving
towards an understanding with Kruschev, Adenauer will be
forced to shift his main reliance to France'.[28] While Kissinger may be right in holding that the de Gaulle–Adenauer
treaty of January 1963 concluded shortly after de Gaulle's
veto of Britain's entry into the Communities was presha-
dowed by their exchanges of 1957, it is also true that de
Gaulle did not succeed in detaching Germany from its
reliance ultimately upon American strength to balance Soviet power, no more than Britain could Germany be part of
an organisation intended to weaken American influence
upon or interest in Europe. That issue would only arise in
the 1980s after the so-called 'end of the "Cold War" '.

Britain, in Kissinger's view, had accepted 'permanent
subordination to American policy' in the hope of having
influence in Washington.[29] In this respect he believes they
were successful: 'British leaders of both parties managed to
make themselves so indispensable to the American decision-
making process that presidents and their entourages came to
regard consultations with London not as a special favour
towards a weaker ally but as a vital component of their own
government.'[30]

However true this may be – and cooperation in some
fields, particularly nuclear matters and intelligence, bound
Britain to the United States in ways not equally open to
other European countries – the basic American view that a
Europe including Britain and linked with the United States

in some form of transatlantic partnership was never abandoned. Indeed Kissinger himself as Nixon's Secretary of
State was to revive 'some of the spirit of Kennedy's approach on the basis of more modest proposals', only for the
idea to founder on 'the old rock of Gaullist opposition'.[31]

By the time Kissinger launched his 'Year of Europe'
Britain was already part of the European Community. But
Britain's decision to opt for membership had not been the
result of American pressure but of a changed attitude to its
own prospects involving a repudiation of the historical
continuity of its European policy, and again largely affected
for both Macmillan, the unsuccessful applicant, and Edward
Heath, the successful one, by their interpretation of the
events of the preceding half-century – Macmillan having
fought in the First World War and opposed 'appeasement'
in the 1930s, and Heath having fought in the Second World
War.

Britain's involvement in both wars with their consequent
human and material losses was seen as an inevitable consequence of successive German challenges to her world position prefaced by a German hegemony in continental
Europe. In the interwar period the ability to build up a
countervailing force had been diminished by the challenge
of a different kind presented by the Soviet Union's sponsor-
ship of revolutionary and subversive movements against all
existing political structures with for much of the time the
British Empire as a primary target. Neither the nineteenth-
century version of a Concert of Powers nor the earlier ideas
of a balance of power could easily be pursued in these
circumstances. The idea of subordinating the states of
Europe to some overarching federal authority which had
attracted thinkers of various kinds for over three centuries
did not have much appeal to Britain which saw the problem
in global rather than continental terms.[32]

Since the European federalists' idea was not merely to
preserve the peace but to regain for Europe a place in the
world it was thought to have lost to external powers, even
they did not see how imperial Britain could be fitted in. The
scheme for a European Union propounded by Count

Coudenhove-Kalergi in his book *Pan-Europe* published in
1923 excluded both the Soviet Union and the British Isles.
On the other hand the vague and ultimately abortive
scheme launched by the French statesman Aristide Briand
in 1929 necessarily included Britain since it was to be
limited to European members of the League of Nations, thus
also excluded the Soviet Union. This proposal, which
seemed to many observers merely a way of strengthening
French hegemony on the continent, did not offer any
practical advantages and was overshadowed by more immediate concerns of both an economic and a political nature.[33]

By the time such ideas were revived after the war, the
United Nations had come into existence and even for those
in Britain who had sympathy for some kind of European
organisation, it was seen as a regional grouping within the
United Nations system. In his Zürich speech on 19 September 1946, Churchill did indeed refer to Briand and the work
of the Pan-European Union, the organisation set up by
Coudenhove-Kalergi (which had incidentally attracted the
favourable attention of the American Congress). The main
ideological impetus had come from resistance circles in
occupied Europe who, while waiting for their liberation by
external powers, could understandably console themselves
for their current powerlessness with utopian notions about a
new political beginning. Since Britain was not occupied and
since most of its men of ideas were in the forces or
government service, echoes of this kind of thinking were
fairly faint.

Indeed the founding of the European Movement in 1948
was not so much the product of such speculation as the
point at which speculation passed into action because for
quite practical reasons governments in that part of Europe
outside the Soviet domain found the idea of Europe a useful
one for giving their objectives potential appeal in quarters
which might otherwise have been tempted to see the Soviet
model as a more desirable one. In Britain, which had fewer
worries on this score and where the agenda of the 1945
Labour government was based on an assessment of Britain's
own requirements in economic and security matters, no

such appeal was felt to be necessary. Proposals emanating from other countries could be judged on their merits.

It must not be overlooked then or later that a federal solution of Europe's problems had significance for the states involved internally as well as externally. Here again there was a difference. Of the nation states of western Europe in addition to Britain only France, the Netherlands, Spain and Portugal have national histories predating the nineteenth century. Germany and Italy were products of that century's national movements; and Germany was now divided. Spain and Portugal were not closely affected by 'European' ideas or organisations until later. In other words, all political arrangements west of the 'iron curtain' seemed in 1945 to be tentative and open to change. Britain did not see itself as falling into that category.

Finally, there was the overriding issue of defence. It had been common in the interwar years to see the advantages of Britain's island position as having been put at threat by the advent of the aircraft. Yet in the Second World War, no invader had landed on these shores; once again it appeared that the silver sea had served it . . .

> in the office of a wall,
> Or as a moat defensive to a house,
> Against the envy of less happier lands.
>
> (Shakespeare, *King Richard II*, i, 40ff)

It was not an asset to be parted with lightly. Defence as well as trade pointed to the importance of Britain's island status. When de Gaulle said that Britain would always prefer the open sea, he had every reason to believe he was right. What needs to be examined is how far British governments were prepared to go to prove him wrong.

Two further questions arise. Is it true to say as is often done that Britain twice 'missed' the bus, that if Britain had been willing to enter the Coal and Steel Community in 1950 or become one of the original signatories to the Treaty of Rome in 1957 after taking part in the discussions leading up to it, the thrust of the Communities could have been directed in a way which would have given them a decided tilt in Britain's direction? And both in respect to this early period and with reference to the developments later on, what grounds did Britain have for believing that it could persuade its continental partners of the superior validity of its own approach? What bargaining counters did it possess?

3 Federalism and Federalists

In order to see what the argument over the European policies of successive British governments has been it is necessary to make clear that it is not a matter of denying the importance to Britain, economically, culturally or militarily, of her nearest neighbours. The point at issue is that the particular approach of Jean Monnet and those who accepted his lead or followed in his footsteps involved the creation of 'supranational' institutions that would in the end transfer power from the nation states of pre-war Europe to a single federal government with the full attributes of a government including legislative, executive and judicial power.[1] It was the unwillingness of British statesmen and officials and of other powerful elements in public life to make this clear that leads one to question either the range of their understanding or their sincerity.

It is not as though the ultimate objective was in any way a secret. If ever H. G. Wells's idea of 'an open conspiracy' was given shape, this was it. And to know what was going on, it was not even necessary to follow the discussions taking place on the continent. There was no lack of voices in Britain itself among those favourable to the whole enterprise ready to explain the implications of what was happening. In a book published in 1994, a well-known British propagandist for European integration wrote: 'the European Union has advanced quite far along the federal road towards a European Union which is its ultimate objective.'[2] At the same time ministers were assuring the British public that the federal road had been abandoned and that the essentials of British sovereignty had been guaranteed by the Treaty of Maastricht.

In fact the question was not an open one. Even before the extension and strengthening of the powers of the European institutions had been given a further impetus by the Single

31

European Act and the Treaty of Maastricht, the essentials
of a federal system were already in place. In joining the
European Communities on 1 January 1973, Britain was in
fact subordinating its own entitlement to self-government to
become a unit within what was already a federal system, in
that legislative powers, including aspects of finance, judicial
powers including deciding what legislation was valid in
Britain, and commercial policy were all now a matter for
institutions in which Britain itself had of necessity only a
minority voice.

Of course this is not to say that Britain in the post-1945
period was a wholly independent actor on the international
scene. Its strength, economic and military, was limited, as is
the lot of all countries – it was also to take part in a number
of international organisations and alliances which limited its
freedom of action and it was still bound up with a network
of relationships within what was still called the British
Commonwealth.[3] But to say that a country's freedom of
action is limited by material consideration and force of
circumstances is not the same as saying that it has ceased to
be a free actor because it is part of a wider grouping to
which important aspects of its sovereignty have been surrendered. And while it is true that even after Maastricht certain
important elements were retained for handling by Britain's
own institutions within intergovernmental agreement –
those in the two 'pillars' – there was abundant evidence
which will be looked at in the final chapter of this book to
show that the protagonists of a 'united Europe' regard the
current phase as only an interim one and have every
intention of pressing on until the federal element is ubiqui-
tous and all-powerful.

It used to be said – and still is in some quarters – that the
British were over-sensitive to the word 'federalism' since it
had a different meaning on the continent to that current in
the English-speaking world where most of the successful
examples of federalism in practice are to be found. But this
is nonsense.[4] If people talked about a 'United States of
Europe' they knew perfectly well what federalism meant.
Nor does a country need to have a federal constitution to

appreciate the substance of the idea.[5] What was true when the process began with the Schuman Plan was that only two countries on the continent (leaving aside the Soviet Union) were themselves governed under federal systems – Switzerland and the new German Federal Republic. Switzerland for many reaons was *sui generis* and took no part at any stage in European 'construction', preserving at once its sovereignty and its neutrality. Germany, which was to become the pivotal country in the European Communities, is a more relevant and complicated case.

While some element of federalism had been present in earlier stages of German constitutional development, the constitution of the Federal Republic was largely the product of American influences as the United States passed from being an occupying power to being an ally. It was of course very different from the American Constitution itself since it was of the parliamentary rather than the presidential variety. Nevertheless it did in some respects resemble the US model. The Länder, like the American states, have no external attributes of sovereignty – they cannot enter into treaties, levy armed forces, issue their own currencies, or make their own arrangements in the sphere of foreign trade. The power to raise taxes and determine totals of public expenditure is even more centralised than has come to be the case in the United States.[6]

There are two aspects of the system which are of particular importance in the European context. In the first place there are precise arrangements for distributing the proceeds of taxation so that there is an automatic transfer of resources from the wealthier to the poorer *Länder*. In the absence of such a formula in the European Community, the Germans have been content to go along with the payment of all receipts to the centre with redistribution being the effect of expenditure programmes of various kinds. In the second place, while the US Senate, whatever the original intentions of the founders, is not the principal means today by which the interests of the states are upheld against the federal government, the Bundesrat in Germany, representing as it does the governments in power in each of the *Länder*, is a formidable weapon in their hands as also is their representation on the board of the Bundesbank. One could add that the system has been shown to be extremely well-adapted to territorial expansion; after the collapse of the German Democratic Republic following upon the withdrawal of Soviet support, the provinces embraced were incorporated without too much difficulty in the framework provided by the West's federal constitution.[7]

While it is true that Belgium has become a rather loose-knit federal state and while experiments with regionalism have been made in post-Mussolini Italy and post-Franco Spain, it remains the case that federal experience on the continent outside Switzerland and Germany is very limited. It would not be a matter for wonder if the German Constitution affected the shape of the existing European institutions and served as a model for their proposed development.

In Britain the idea of federalism was more widely understood and appreciated. The United States itself is much more deeply studied in Britain than in continental Europe. Although Britain, apart from the brief vogue for 'home rule all round' in the years just before the First World War, had not itself toyed with the notion of a federal structure, the idea of federation as applied to the Empire–Commonwealth retained its devotees until the 1930s. And in Canada, Australia and, though with many differences, India as well, there were successful examples of federations within the Commonwealth orbit. British officials and politicians were forced to look closely at what federal systems might imply during the unsuccessful attempts to create federations in the Caribbean and Central Africa in the period of decolonisation. Indeed Harold Macmillan was more concerned about the possibilities of federation in Central Africa at a time when he attempted to get Britain into the European Communities than with the proper analysis of what such membership would entail.

Nor can it be said that the so-called absence of a 'written constitution' in the United Kingdom meant that British lawyers knowing the role of the Privy Council as a final

court of appeal in the Commonwealth were unaware of the
kind of decisions that the existence of federal systems
imposes upon the judiciary.

In retrospect the inability to analyse the nature of what
was being created in Brussels, Luxembourg and Strasbourg
remains mysterious. It is true that when the Schuman Plan
was launched and subsequently also, the word used to
describe such creations was 'supranational' rather than
federal. International in the aftermath of a dreadful war was
an appealing notion. And 'supranational' sounded very like
'international'. Indeed some important figures in British
public life continued into the 1990s to talk as though there
was some comparison to be drawn between Britain's international obligations and her membership of the European
Union.

There should have been a warning from another source.
The Council of Europe was undoubtedly an international
rather than a supranational organisation and one which
owed much to British initiative.[8] Yet by accepting the
Human Rights Convention of the Council and by permitting from 1966 the right of direct recourse to it by British
citizens, the country had familiarised itself with a situation
in which individual cases before British courts could be
settled by a foreign tribunal to whose decisions successive
governments felt themselves obliged to conform.[9]

International conventions governing some aspects of domestic policy were nothing new, nor were the organisations
through which such conventions were arrived at limited to
Europe. Membership of such organisations and the implementation of such conventions were clearly compatible
with national sovereignty in a way which was not true of a
unit within a federal system. The essence of a federal system
lies in the division of legislative powers between a federal
authority and the authorities of the units of which it is
composed – German *Länder*, American states, Canadian
provinces and so forth. Federal laws in some spheres must
have a direct impact upon the individual citizen and be
interpreted in the last resort by the federal judicature. By
this criterion the Schuman Plan, Euratom and the Common

Market were the basis for a federal system, in being when British membership was accepted and subsequently carried forward towards the goal of a fully fledged government of Europe by the Single European Act and the Treaty of Maastricht.

One reason for the failure to understand the process may be that it was embodied both in Community legislation and the interpretation of that legislation by the European Court of Justice. If the legal literature on the process had been studied the federal aspect could not have been overlooked, but for the most part, British politicians and civil servants have been too ready to take what are called 'pragmatic' views, that is to say, to consider the short-range impact of the Community upon individual aspects of trade rather than the long-term impact upon the country's capacity for self-government.[10] What is perhaps more surprising, as already noted, is that so few notes of warning have been sounded from the ranks of the British legal profession itself, Lords Denning and Diplock being notable exceptions.

British lawyers must have been aware even before they came across the issues dealt with in the European Court of Human Rights and the European Court of Justice that there were profound and well-known differences between the two legal families into which the nations of Europe had been divided ever since the twelfth century. On the continent, lawyers were trained for their tasks in the law faculties of universities whose goal was 'a judicial science common to all and adapted to the conditions of the modern world'. A second family was that of the common law including the law of England. Since the time of the enlightenment in Europe the continental tradition has been carried into effect largely through the enactment of codes of which the French Code Napoléon is the classic example. Judges brought up in this tradition — and many members of the Court have been law professors rather than judges in their own country — look to the matching of cases to the requirements of codes. But 'Common Law is altogether different in its characteristics, as it was formed primarily by judges who had to resolve specific disputes'.[11] There are of course other differences.

Continental tradition has been more favourable to judicial review of administrative decisions.[12] Since only Ireland among the other members of the Community has a common law system, it is obvious that judges from that system will always be heavily outnumbered in the European courts. Nevertheless it is still worth speculating as to why it was that so few alarm bells were sounded from within the British legal world as to the extent to which Britain's own courts were being demoted as the input of Community law became greater.[13] Sir Patrick Neill and a number of younger barristers provide some exceptions to this general acquiescence.

It is of course difficult to separate the impact of law, in this case Community law, from its political and social context. The acceptability of laws depends upon confidence in the manner by which they are arrived at. Where unanimity prevails in the Council of Ministers, the legislature of the Communities, the interests of an individual country are preserved; when it is a matter of voting even by a 'qualified majority', the possibility of being outvoted always exists, and with it the possibility of laws being adopted that run counter to a particular country's interests or aspirations. Furthermore there is not always clarity about the borderline between the political and the legal. The most obvious example of this is the sudden eruption into the discussions of European integration of the word 'subsidiarity'. This found a place in the preamble to the Treaty of Maastricht when it was stated that the states 'were resolved to continue the process of creating an ever closer union among the peoples of Europe in which decisions are taken as closely as possible to the citizen in accordance with the principle of subsidiarity'. And this was further explained in a new Article 3b:

> In areas which do not fall within its exclusive competence, the Community shall take action, in accordance with the principle of subsidiarity, only if and only so far as the proposed action cannot be sufficiently achieved by the Member States and can, therefore, by reason of the scale or effects of the proposed action, be better achieved by the Community.

British ministers made much of this insertion as though it represented a barrier to the further expansion of the powers of the Community, and so was somehow an obstacle to the growth of federalism.

Yet it is nothing of the kind. A well-known French commentator on international affairs put it bluntly: 'there is no logical difference between the principle of subsidiarity and that of federalism. Either states remain sovereign or they surrender their sovereignty by degrees.'[14]

Subsidiarity is not a legal concept and its inclusion in the treaty does not invite legal interpretation. It is simply a guide to the making of political decisions by the Community's institutions as to where particular aspects of governmental activity should be allocated. It was made abundantly clear by the Commission at the time of the Edinburgh summit in December 1992 that the commitment to subsidiarity was in no way intended to act as a brake upon the Commission's initiatives in the legislative field. While there was later some retreat on minor points from areas of activity formerly claimed by the Commission, this did no more than indicate where the initiative would lie. Matters lying within the 'exclusive competence' of the Community were excluded by the wording of the treaty itself and the tenor of the Court's decisions had been to enlarge the scope of such matters by ruling out concurrent jurisdiction. States were simply elbowed out of successive areas of activity. And given the other guiding principle of the *acquis communautaire* that anything the Community has once taken in hand remains with it permanently, the idea that there was or could be a retreat from federalism was an illusion – one among many.

No doubt there are verbal traps when one is dealing with countries which operate and think in different languages. 'Subsidiarity' is a concept drawn from Roman Catholic theology. It was hardly common currency among British parliamentarians and officials when Jacques Delors used it in his first presidential speech to the European Parliament.[15] Sometimes foreigners can make heavy weather of expressions used in another country. Timothy Garton Ash, no stranger to Germany, has pointed out that the German Constitutional Court has defined the European Union as a 'Staatenbund', and says that this is hard to translate into English. Yet 'Staatenbund' has always been seen as the German equivalent of 'confederation' – and although the Swiss use of confederation to describe what is now an essentially federal system is misleading the nuance is not hard to detect.[16] The role of the German Constitutional Court in the definition of the Community's competence is, as will be seen, not without importance, so the point is worth taking.

A final distinction between British and continental perceptions of the law is harder to define but may in practice be no less significant. A large part of the legislation emanating from Brussels is in the form of directives which national legislation has to transpose into detailed provisions. Continental civil servants are as we have seen inclined to see their task as involving the recognition of particular local circumstances.

When businesses complain of the dire effects of some Community legislation or the ordinary citizen sees evidence of the sillinesses that result from the drive for harmonisation – in weights and measures for instance – it is often alleged by Europhiles that Brussels is not to blame, just over-zealous British officialdom. But the defence is a weak one, since it is an inevitable consequence of the British attitudes towards law that are being exploited for Community purposes. People who travel can of course observe that much Community legislation, particularly where it concerns traditional behaviour in respect of food and drink, is cheerfully disregarded in foreign countries. It helps to make the point that uniformity of legislation across national boundaries except where directly required to implement genuine international agreements is bound to cause aggravation rather than promote ever closer union. And of course this feature of the scene is supplemented by the conviction that many aspects of Community rules are designed not for some overarching common good but to promote particular private interests in the countries which tend to set the tone in Brussels, either because they are themselves powerful like Germany or because their support is needed for other aspects of the policies of the major countries.

It is possible to view the growth of the Community's area of activity and claims in terms of an even progression towards a new legal order. But that should not be at the expense of seeing what interests – apart from those of the European Commission itself and its employees – are at the same time being promoted.

It may be the case that in some countries it is the confidence that their officialdom can cope with any possible adverse effects of Community legislation that explains the very minor role that has hitherto been accorded to the role of national parliaments. Britain has a fairly elaborate machinery in both Houses of Parliament to see that ministers are given guidance as to the line they should take in dealing with Commission drafts likely to come before them. But with the exception of Denmark and the Netherlands there seem few continental parallels to such exhaustive supervision of Community activity by national parliaments.[17] Nor are the partisans of integration much concerned to promote such interest since their hope has always been to make the European Parliament one of the principal organs of the Communities (now the Union), fulfilling for Europe the role of democratic control that national parliaments fulfil in respect of their own home governments.

In the light of all such evidence it is impossible to deny that what we have in the European Community (now the European Union) is a federal system of which the United Kingdom has been a member since the coming into force of the Treaty of Accession. The fact that the Community has over the periods preceding that decision and following upon it increased the scope of its activities at the expense of the member states is not in itself surprising. The phenomenon is not uncommon in the history of federations nor are the ways in which this expansion has been brought about: judicial decisions and formal revisions of the original documents. The constitutional history of the United States is the *locus classicus* for such developments though there change has not been all in the same direction.[18] It is also the case that in the early years in Europe there were setbacks as when the failure to create a European Defence Community led to the abandonment of proposals for a European Political Community which was to have been its complement.

What is unique about the European experience is something different. From the very beginning there was a powerful group of politicians in the countries of the Six for whom the ultimate goal was a United States of Europe in which the weight of authority would come to rest with the institutions at the centre. For this point of view a sounding-board was provided by the Assembly, later through direct elections to become a Parliament and itself a contender for power. More important however has been the role of the two major bodies, the Commission and the Court. Both bodies have regarded their tasks as not merely the transaction of day-to-day business – the idea that the Commission is some kind of 'civil service' is hard to eradicate from British minds – but also and more importantly as promoting the movement towards an expansion of the Community's powers and the enhancement of the authority of its institutions. As has been stated often enough the Court takes a teleological view of its functions, and is as unlike the Judicial Committee of the House of Lords, or the French Conseil d'Etat or the German Constitutional Court, as it is possible to conceive. The fact that the Council of Ministers is the legislative body – though able to act only on proposals from the Commission – has not seriously detracted from the process, the more so since in some of the governments the ministers have themselves been favourable to the federalist tendency, and that where there is majority voting, ministers who are not can do nothing about it.

Since what the Commission does is covered by ministerial authority – even when the ministers' own decisions have been prompted by their permanent representatives at Brussels – it is through the successive decisions by the Court that the strengthening of the federal yoke can best be followed. Again there is nothing new in this. No specific provision for the exercise of judicial review appears in the US Constitution, yet by his decision in 1819 in *McCulloch* v. *Maryland*, Chief Justice Marshall limited the jurisdiction of the states to the benefit of the federal authority. It shows that what a court can bring about may be by the exercise of a negative power – not saying what the federal authority can do but what the authority within the unit cannot. The powers of the European Court in this respect were not specifically laid down in the Treaty of Rome but its negative powers have proved amply sufficient to drive the federal chariot along. The key was originally Article 177 which gave national courts the duty of referring to the European Court questions of Community law arising in cases coming before them, as well as Articles 169 and 170 which allowed the Commission or member states to proceed against states that failed to observe their obligations under the treaty.

The record makes it impossible to dissent from Sir Patrick Neill's view that 'under the authority conferred upon it by these and other provisions the EJC has interpreted the Treaty and the acts of the institutions in a way that has carried community law far beyond the written text of the various instruments'.[19]

As with any other court the principles laid down in dealing with a specific case will then be adhered to in subsequent cases which are held to fall under the same general heading. Only a few cases need therefore be considered to establish the extent to which the authority of the Communities has been enlarged.

It is important to note that some of these decisions had been made before the accession of the United Kingdom so that there was no excuse for the government not to know what kind of organisation it was entering. In 1963 in the *Van Gend en Loos* case where a private company accused the government of the Netherlands of violating Article 12 of the Treaty of Rome, the Court held that the treaty applied to the citizens of the member states, not merely to their governments, and hence created for those citizens legal rights as well as obligations. It was this aspect of the judgment which makes it possible to argue that the treaty has direct effects without the need for implementing action by the member states so that strictly speaking the British European Communities Act of 1972 was unnecessary. The Court stated the position by declaring that 'the Community constitutes a new legal order of international law for the benefit of which the states have limited their sovereign rights albeit within limited fields and the subjects of which comprise not only Member States but also their nationals'. It is worth noting that the Court, following the further claims of Community competence stretching well beyond the need to ensure freedom of trade within a Common Market, altered in 1991 the formula 'within limited fields' to 'within ever wider fields' (Opinion 1/91 *Re a Draft Treaty on a European Economic Area*). In a somewhat similar case (Case 6/64 *Costa v. ENEL*) the Court upheld the primacy of Community law over Italian domestic law, made subsequent to the treaty. In talking of

> a Community of unlimited duration, having its own institutions, its own personality and capacity of representation on the international plane and more particularly real powers stemming from a limitation of sovereignty or a transfer of powers from the States to the Community and in declaring them the Member States have limited their sovereign rights, albeit within limited fields, and have thus created a body of law which binds both their nationals and themselves

the Court made plain its commitment to a single legal system covering the entire Community:

> The integration into the laws of each Member State of provisions which derive from the Community, and more generally the *terms and spirit of the Treaty* [sic], make it impossible for the States, as a corollary, to accord precedence to a unilateral and subsequent measure over a legal system accepted by them on the basis of reciprocity.

It might also be suggested that the fact that Community law is held to bind individuals directly provided a legal foundation for the creation of a 'European citizenship' in the Treaty of Maastricht with all the consequences that this entails.

A further point that has become apparent is that once an area of governmental activity has come to be seen as affecting a responsibility of the Community, individual governments wishing to legislate have to await the agreement of all members. An example is to be found in the field of safety measures affecting motor coaches. No country seems to be prepared to say that it must put the safety of its own citizens within its own borders first. If Britain were to do this the Europhile argument that 'sovereignty' is a mere word would be put to the test.

In 1970 the Court further decided that Community law did not only override the ordinary laws of the member states but was even superior to their constitutions, even where these embodied guarantees of fundamental rights as in Germany (Case 11/70 *Internationale Handsgesellschaft mbH v. Einfuhr-und Vorratstele für Getreide und Futtermittel*): 'Respect for fundamental rights forms an integral part of the general principles of law protected by the Court of Justice. The protection of such rights, whilst inspired by the constitutional traditions common to Member States must be ensured within the framework of the structure and objectives of the community.' The Court has in subsequent decisions made its point by claiming to have incorporated the European Convention of Human Rights into its own jurisprudence within the areas to which Community action applies.

The perceptible but still to some extent limited degree of federalism which Britain accepted by accession to the treaty has subsequently been given a further bias in a centralist direction by a series of Court decisions as well as by the provisions of the Single European Act and the Treaty of Maastricht. Not only, as already noted, was the British judiciary apparently indifferent to the diminution of its authority but the presence of British advocates-general and judges in the Luxembourg Court seems to have made no difference to the general direction of the Court's jurisprudence. 'Going native' has seemed as attractive in Luxembourg as in Brussels.[20]

The general structure of Community legislation according to Article 189 of the treaty had been through 'regulations' 'decisions' and 'directives'. It was stated in the standard texts that while 'regulations' and 'decisions' were directly binding, 'directives' gave the objective to be reached but left it to the individual states to choose the form in which it should be applied. In 1974 (*Yvonne Van Duyn* v. *Home Office*) it was decided that this distinction need not apply and that litigants could appeal to the language of a directive even when no effect had been given to it by legislation in the country concerned. And this was extended to bodies such as professional associations which had public functions even though they would not themselves have been able to do anything about bringing the directive into effect through the enactment of domestic law.

In a case in 1991 (Cases 6/90 and 9/90), *Andrea Francovich and Others* v. *Italian Republic*, it was held that individuals could sue a government for damages if the non-implementation of a directive deprived them of rights they would have had under its provisions.

While other illustrations of the extension of the Court's scope of action could be given from the point of view of the United Kingdom, the principal case is *Factortame* in which a specific provision of the British Merchant Shipping Act of 1988 which prevented foreign ship-owners registering in Britain so as to get round the quotas imposed by the Common Fisheries Policy was overruled by the European Court.[21] The acceptance of this ruling meant that the basic principle of British law, the sovereignty of Parliament, had been publicly abandoned. Its political sensitivity was the greater because the control of merchant shipping was of primary importance to a country whose historic destiny had been on the sea. It was also felt that the preservation of fish stocks which was one of the objectives of the Common Fisheries Policy was one of those aspects of Community legislation that the British were more rigorous about than some other member states. The case goes some way to explaining why, in the dispute over fisheries policy between Spain and Canada in 1995, British sentiment was almost entirely on Canada's side.

In direct resistance to the expansion of Community powers through the Court, Britain has had little to go on as far as other member states were concerned.

In France, while the Cour de Cassation found no difficulty in accepting the primacy of Community law, the Conseil d'Etat, the Court dealing with public law issues, showed itself originally opposed to the idea that French legislation could be invalidated by reference to Community law but in later cases it has tended to go along with Community law including the direct effectiveness of Community directives.[22] Italian action has been somewhat parallel to the French example.[23]

The most important case, already referred to, is that of Germany where for understandable reasons the status of the Constitution and of the rights it guarantees are of particular significance. The decision in 1974 was modified in a case in 1986 when the Court decided that it would no longer examine the compatibility of Community legislation with German fundamental rights while the European Court continued to protect rights. It also accepted the unmediated effect of directives.[24]

It may be that the issue where Germany is concerned is still open. Increasing political awareness in Germany of some aspects of the development of the Union notably in relation to the 'single currency' may attract attention to the provisions of the Constitution. An interpretation by the German Constitutional Court on 11 October 1993 of the Maastricht Treaty has been held to invalidate Germany's ratification, and although the German government has behaved as though it had ratified the treaty it is possible that the issue could become a live one again.

In his oral evidence to the House of Lords Committee on 26 June 1995, Sir Patrick Neill quoted a recent lecture by a judge of the German Constitutional Court which suggests that these issues are not entirely closed:

If in an adjudication of the European Court of Justice the judges were not only to apply their judicial skill in interpreting the Treaty, but also extended the latter in some substantive respect, this legal instrument would not be valid on German territory for the constitutional reason that German official bodies would be prevented from applying the legal instrument in Germany. Accordingly the German Federal Constitutional Court examines legal instruments of the European Court of Justice in order to ascertain whether they lie within the limits of the duties and powers contractually delegated to this court or whether they overstep them.[25]

Such a view, which suggests parity between two legal systems and their courts, is incompatible with federalism and we would be back to a 'Staatenbund' or 'confederation'. But the opinion of one judge is not enough on which to build expectations for the future.

More immediately of concern is how the provision of the Maastricht Treaty (Article 171) enabling states to be fined for refusing to comply with decisions made against them by the Court will work in practice. It is perhaps ironical that the government of the UK which was so concerned to distance itself from further steps in the federal direction should have pushed for this clause.[26] Just as with the Single European Act, the United Kingdom favoured the extension of qualified majority voting in the belief that it would only be used to speed up the creation of the Single Market, so again some idea of penalising countries less punctilious than Britain about implementing European law may have blinded Britain's negotiators to the constitutional implications of such a provision.

What is clear is that by 1995, Britain was part of a federal system whose two leading members, far from wishing to see powers returned to the member states, were bent on further centralisation as Chapter 7 will make plain.

From the point of view of the argument about federalism, the most important new feature was the pressure towards economic and monetary union (EMU) embodied in the 'single currency'. Once again, the British government seemed to have missed the point. In the first place, its advocates on the continent had always made it plain that

EMU was an important step towards the total submergence of individual states in the new federal structures. But even if this evidence was ignored, the abandonment of control over one's currency was clearly to abandon any pretensions to independence. A currency can only be credible if backed by a government.

As any historian is aware, the creation through coinage of a medium of exchange has always been an important ingredient of sovereignty. Indeed historians of the ancient world or the Middle Ages are much indebted to numismatists. The coming of paper money enhanced rather than diminished governmental responsibility.

The British 'opt-out' at Maastricht was based on the assumption that the argument was a purely economic one and that a decision as to whether or not to join in creating a single currency could be determined by economic conditions at the time when a decision would have to be made. A similar blindness affected the leaders of the opposition parties. So activity was focused on the location of the new European monetary institutions and the design of coins and banknotes. In this way public attention was diverted from the real issues to worrying about whether the Queen's likeness would appear on banknotes as though this could matter once yet another element of self-government had been removed from the Queen's subjects.

Once again one wonders whether politicians who argued that it was possible to have a single currency and retain separate sovereign governments believed what they were saying or whether they were determined to conceal the truth in order to cajole their fellow-citizens yet further into the European morass. Or were there some individuals of one kind and some of the other?

After all one did not need to be a historian to see the obvious. Every existing federal country – the United States, Canada, Australia, India, Germany, Switzerland – leaves currency matters to the federal institutions and denies these powers to the different units. How otherwise could they function as economic entities? Why should a European federation be any different? How could it be?

The question became more difficult to answer when, in the latter part of 1995, questions about the single currency began to dominate debate in the continental countries that had seemed keenest on the idea. No one had done more to bring the single currency into the centre of debate on closer union than Jacques Delors.[27] Yet Delors himself now admitted that he thought the proposals for political union in the Maastricht Treaty had been pushed too far and blamed the Germans for insisting on political union on Adenauer's lines as the price of abandoning the Deutschmark.[28] Yet this would suggest that Delors, who believed that a single currency was necessary to sustain the single market, also believed that one could have a currency which had no governmental authority to control and sanction it. If Delors was oblivious to the logic of federalism, who could be expected to understand it?

4 Europe in British Politics 1945–75

The idea of a solution to Europe's problems through the creation of some form of United States of Europe was, as has been seen, the outcome of particular circumstances which Britain had thankfully avoided. In so far as there was planning for the postwar world in government circles, it took for granted that while Britain had traditional interests in what happened in Europe, particularly in the avoidance of a continental hegemony, it would approach such problems with the interests of the Empire–Commonwealth and relations with the United States given at least equal weight.

No doubt in more dangerous circumstances, more radical ideas might have come to the fore. In the crisis of June 1940, Churchill had not put aside the idea that France might remain a belligerent, if only from its overseas territories, if her future could be guaranteed as part of an Anglo-French union. This would, had it ever materialised, have produced a higher degree of integration than was to be the case with the original European Communities. It could indeed be argued that despite their earlier rivalries and collisions of interest overseas, the two countries which had twice gone to war as allies in the space of a quarter of a century were more natural partners than France and Germany. But it was not to be.[1] The Vichy government accepted the suzerainty of the German Reich and when a different France emerged under de Gaulle's leadership, it was to seek where possible to differentiate itself from the 'Anglo-Saxon' world.

Churchill himself believed that there were more important things for his government to do than to occupy itself with the postwar settlement. In so far as he had general ideas as to the shape the new Europe should take, it was for Britain and the USSR and indeed the Americans to stay aloof, forming the leading core of the United Nations, while

51

there should be within the organisation some 'European Instrument' – which he thought of as confederal in style.[2] It is clear that Britain would not form part of a specifically European entity. Within the Foreign Office, greater prominence was also given to the proposed world organisation. The main problem was seen as preventing a renewal of German aggression. A United Nations Commission for Europe should include Britain as well as the USSR and the United States and could eventually develop into a 'Council of Europe': 'a Council of Europe in which the United Kingdom, the United States of America and the U.S.S.R. did not play an active part might become in the course of time an instrument through which Germany could recover peacefully that hegemony over Europe which she has momentarily established by force of arms during the present war'.[3]

It is worth seeing what Foreign Office expectations were since while Churchill himself was out of power when the decisions about Europe's future came to be made, the personnel of the Foreign Office provided a direct line of continuity between the Churchill–Eden regime and the Attlee–Bevin regime that succeeded it. On the other hand there were assumptions in the earlier thinking, such as that in the document of July 1943 just quoted, which the course of events was to falsify. By the time of the Potsdam Conference in July 1945 during which the change in British representation took place, fears about the distant prospect of a revival of German hegemony gave way to fears about the intentions of the Soviet Union, as Germany itself entered upon its long decades of partition. The expectation of close American cooperation in maintaining the peace in Europe also seemed less probable and was indeed only to be revived by the Soviet threat and the ensuing 'Cold War'.

In the immediate aftermath of Potsdam, priority was given to relations with France as the most likely partner in dealing with the problems Britain was having to face as the occupying power in the heart of industrial Germany. Eleven days after returning from Potsdam, Bevin argued for 'extensive political and military co-operation throughout Western

Europe, with an Anglo-French alliance as the cornerstone'.[4]
This line of thinking became entangled with the concept of
a 'Third Force' which had much support in Labour circles
at the time in an effort to create a European entity not
dependent upon either the Soviet Union or the United
States. But the whole venture ran into obstacles especially in
the fact that France had its own objectives in Germany
which would have had the effect of permanently weakening
her, while Britain was even then alive to the possible future
need to involve Germany in a balance against future Soviet
expansionism. The French saw no need to compromise on
this or other issues separating the two governments since
they believed that 'Britain needed France more than France
needed Britain' and that 'given time, the British would
accept much of the French position'.[5]

In any event the 'Third Force' idea did not hold the stage
for long. It was predicated on the belief that the United
States was indifferent to the problems of Britain and Europe
and that its support could not be depended upon. By the
first half of 1947, increasing friction with the Soviet Union
led the United States to confirm its interest in the future of
Europe through the Marshall Plan and the OEEC and all
British thinking assumed that any new organisation in
western Europe would require United States support.[6] On
the other hand, the United States differed from Britain in
the determination it showed from the beginning of the
OEEC to view Britain's role essentially as part of a common
western European economic bloc and to treat Britain
thenceforward as a regional rather than as a world power
which in Britain's own eyes it still remained.[7]

British policy was directed towards concrete assurances on
the defence side, first in the Anglo-French Treaty of Dun-
kirk of March 1947 and subsequently, what Bevin spoke of
as a 'Western Union', the Brussels Treaty between Britain,
France and the Benelux countries in March 1948. While in
the Anglo-French Treaty, Germany had been named as the
potential aggressor, by 1948 the Soviet threat was the
dominant one in western minds and the Brussels Treaty did
not specify against whom its defence plans were to be

directed.[8] By now it was possible to attempt to create a wider guarantee including the United States and after much negotiation, the North Atlantic Treaty Organisation was formally created by a treaty signed at Washington on 4 April 1949.[9]

The general lines of British policy were widely acceptable except on the Left of the Labour Party which continued to hanker after better relations with the Soviet Union.[10] A smaller minority of politicians were interested in the idea of creating a common political framework within western Europe in which Britain's economic and ultimately its defence arrangements could find a place. It has been argued that Churchill himself belonged to this minority. That is an error based upon picking out only portions of his famous speeches in Zürich on 19 September 1946, London on 18 April 1947 and The Hague on 7 May 1948. A more careful study of the texts and other evidence shows that while Churchill was keen on the idea of a 'United States of Europe' as a means of bringing about a permanent settlement between France and Germany on which he believed future peace would depend, he did not envisage Britain itself being part of any such combination, since its true role lay in its acting as a connecting link between Europe, the British Empire and Commonwealth and the United States.[11]

British policy had already been shown to be diverging from that of its Brussels Pact partners when in October 1948 at a meeting of foreign ministers, Robert Schuman for France supported by Paul-Henri Spaak for Belgium proposed the calling of a European Assembly to explore the possibilities of progress towards European unity. Churchill did indeed criticise Bevin for his reluctance to accept what was admittedly no more than a gesture but this did not indicate any disagreement on fundamentals.[12] Out of these and subsequent discussions there emerged the Council of Europe, an organisation whose statute was agreed upon in London in May 1949 and which embodied the British preference for a wider membership and for intergovernmental as opposed to supranational solutions.[13]

The continental advocates of closer integration were forced back for the moment on the economic road which Jean Monnet believed would eventually entail political union. The first move in this direction was the Schuman Plan for a European Coal and Steel Community. France's insistence that those taking part in the discussions of the plan should commit themselves in advance to pooling their coal and steel resources led to the British refusal to take part, and to the creation of the ECSC without the UK.[14]

The decision taken in May 1950 was criticised by the Opposition including Churchill but no attempt to reverse the outcome was made when the Conservatives returned to power in the following year. The decision was regarded at the time by the Americans and later on by British political figures as a major error and the point at which Britain missed its chance of helping to shape the future of European institutions.[15] Yet given the cast of thought that went to its creation, it is hard to see how any British government, even one in which trade union influence was less strong, could have accepted entering upon such a venture.

It was the military defence of Europe that most preoccupied Churchill and he was by 1949 convinced that Germany would have to take part in it. There were both in Britain and among countries recently occupied by German forces some natural objections to such a course, but after the outbreak of the Korean War, the Americans made it clear that their continued participation in European defence depended upon the willingness of the Europeans to accept a German contribution.[16] The French were willing to accept this only in the context of a European army and the question of whether this should be the next step, and how it should be formed and controlled, took up much of the energy of western diplomacy for some time thereafter. Churchill had argued for such a concept in a speech to the Council of Europe in August 1950 when Germany was already a member but there is no indication that he thought that Britain could join. The proposal for a 'European Defence Community' embodied in a treaty between the ECSC members of 27 May 1952 had received

Churchill's backing in December 1951 but when he visited
Washington in the following month he cast doubt upon the
desirability of a European army – a 'sludgy amalgam' as he
called it.[17]

In the event the European Defence Community treaty
was rejected by the French National Assembly. Eden, the
foreign secretary in the Churchill government, never himself
a friend of European integration, was on this occasion
bound to step in if the damage to western defence was not
to be too severe.[18] The solution to enable Germany to rearm
within an acceptable framework was found by modifying the
Brussels Pact through the inclusion of Germany and Italy
and renaming it the Western European Union, in an
agreement reached in Paris on 23 October 1954. French
assent was secured by a British undertaking to keep a
proportion of its forces on the continent. The core of
Britain's defence thinking still rested on NATO, and the
WEU did not play a memorable role in European politics
until the issues raised by the Maastricht Treaty propelled it
into the limelight.

While the immediate issue of German participation in the
defence of Europe had thus been solved, the WEU. was not
seen as the basis for a European Political Community as the
EDC had been.

Elements in the Six now returned to economic integration
as the route to the fulfilment of the European idea. But the
considerations that led to the creation of the Common
Market, a move largely due to the Dutch, was primarily a
way of solving certain particular problems of the member
countries. These problems and the general gap between
British thinking and what was becoming the common approach elsewhere meant that Britain did not see a direct
interest in such developments. The Conference of the Six at
Messina in June 1955 was followed by detailed discussion in
Brussels to which Britain only sent an 'observer' who
withdrew in November.[19] In May 1956, the Six decided to
proceed with the preparation of treaties to set up a European Economic Community (Common Market) and a European Atomic Authority. The treaties were signed at Rome

on 25 March 1957 and entered into force on 1 January
1958.

Hitherto Britain had been indifferent or hostile to such
moves, unable, as some would believe, to appreciate the
extent to which its industry was falling behind its main
competitors and notably Germany, and giving priority to
seeing the City recover its financial preeminence. Its voice
counted more with Conservative politicians than did industry's. But an alternative policy based upon the sterling area
was frustrated by the unwillingness of the old Commonwealth to fit itself into such a pattern. The other main
objective, as it had been ever since the end of the war, was
to retain some kind of special relationship with the United
States. It was encouraged in the belief that this was possible
by the persistent ambiguity of United States policy towards
Europe. The movement towards political integration had
strong US backing but those responsible for US economic
policy were chary of encouraging what might turn out to be
an area of discrimination against American products. It was
a dichotomy which was to persist but it did not mean that
the Americans would refrain from pressing Britain to join
the new European institutions – on the contrary, as will be
seen, Jean Monnet, uninterested in the Common Market,
was to become the American voice in Europe, his appeal
magnified by his access to American funds.

It is also clear that despite the difficulty of turning the
Commonwealth into the basis for an alternative economic
grouping, its existence and preservation bulked large in
British thinking in the Labour Party as well as among
Conservatives. The series of events summed up in the word
'Suez' affected confidence in the Anglo-American relationship and even more in the reality of the Commonwealth as
a substitute for Empire. 'Suez', in the words of an authority
on Commonwealth history, marked

> a psychological watershed. It led to a hastening of the
> removal of the vestiges of Britain's imperial statehood, a
> diminishing pride in the Commonwealth among Britain's
> relative 'attentive publics' and a willingness to reduce or

shed the role of principal in Commonwealth affairs –
especially if this would facilitate membership in the
European Economic Community.[20]

It was in the Conservative Party where the crisis was most
visible. Until 'Suez' many Conservatives had cherished the
idea that even with its new non-British members the Commonwealth might still form a viable international system on
its own. But the identification by Nehru of India's cause
with that of Nasser destroyed that vision for good.

It has been argued by someone involved in the development in Europe that it was the preoccupation of ministers
with 'Suez' that made them pay too little attention to what
was going on between the Six and the importance of the
transformation in the European scene that was being
brought about in Britain's absence.[21] The shift in the British
reaction took place under the premiership of Harold Macmillan who, although far from accepting the idea that
Britain was simply another European country, was less
instinctively hostile to notions of European integration than
Eden had been and had indeed in 1961 expressed sympathy
with the idea of Britain taking part in some form of
European construction.[22]

Free of the bonds of '*Commonwealth d'abord*', Britain and
the British Conservatives in particular could now adopt the
idea of European unity, hitherto of interest only to a
minority. In this rather negative or roundabout way, Suez
can be seen as a proximate cause of Britain's application to
join the Common Market.[23] On the other hand, Suez was
also a factor in the final collapse of the Fourth Republic and
the coming into power of General de Gaulle which was to
provide for the time being an insurmountable obstacle to
that application.[24] The possibility of some form of association with the Common Market had occupied British policy-makers in the Treasury and Board of Trade even before
attention was diverted for a time by Suez. Whatever the
political differences with major Commonwealth countries, it
had always been clear that trade with the Commonwealth
and the desire to retain the sterling area would be obstacles

to full membership along the lines the Six were discussing. It was also not clear how far the Six themselves would come to a successful conclusion of their negotiations and if it were successful whether the new arrangements would hold. The British government was prone to note the persistence of French protectionism and interventionism despite their undertakings in the OECC, and on the political side, the friction between France and Germany was always likely, it seemed, to become visible again.[25] The upshot was a design for a half-way house in the form of Plan G of 29 September 1956 for a 'partial Free Trade area' consisting of the Customs Union of the Six, United Kingdom and such other members of the OEEC that might wish to join; the Scandinavian countries, Switzerland and Austria were seen as likely members of such an association.[26]

When the British proposals for an industrial free trade area were publicly launched in 1957 it became clear that the Six would not find these acceptable and were more concerned to see that the way was clear for the ratification of the Treaty of Rome and the coming into existence of their Economic Community. In London it was still felt impossible to go the whole way with the Six because of the impact that membership of their proposed community would have on Britain's very different position in respect of agriculture, and its commitments to the Commonwealth in relation to buying their agricultural products. On the other hand, there was among ministers and in Whitehall and the City a reluctance to be left out altogether from the developments on the continent.

In trying to elucidate Macmillan's own shift towards seeking membership in the EEC, it is necessary to recall the fact that the first years of his premiership were a time of marked instability in the wider political world.[27] There were the confrontations between the United States and the USSR over the U-2 affair and the Cuban Missile Crisis. In the Commonwealth, the ending of South Africa's membership and the accelerating tempo of decolonisation in the light of Macmillan's 'wind of change' speech were all calls upon the Prime Minister's time and energy. The fall of the Fourth

Republic in France and the coming back into power of General de Gaulle, his new constitution and the liquidation of France's hold on Algeria provided a new setting for Britain's difficult relations with her closest continental neighbour.

The balance of personalities in the cabinet had also to be taken into account. When Earl Home succeeded Selwyn Lloyd at the Foreign Office in the reshuffle of July 1960, Edward Heath was as Lord Privy Seal entrusted both with the House of Commons aspects of Foreign Office business and with particular responsibility for relations with Europe. His biographer does not believe that he was chosen for this role because of his convictions about the development of policy towards the EEC, which were strengthened in the course of the negotiations in which he was destined to take a leading part.[28] But it cannot be unimportant that he was to show himself almost alone among leading British politicians – certainly until much later on the Conservative side – in being influenced by the kind of dedication to European integration usually found only among continental statesmen. His experiences as a soldier and as someone who had attended the Nuremberg War Crimes Trials had made him see the safeguarding of peace as the major task of his generation. He had also early on taken the view that while Soviet Russia was the obvious immediate threat, it was not possible to rule out the possibility of a future aggressive Germany. His primary purpose in advocating European integration was the containment of Germany and this helped to make him understanding of French views on the subject as he made clear as early as the debate on Britain's rejection of the Schuman Plan.[29]

Reginald Maudling, the paymaster-general, was appointed as the minister to coordinate British policy on European matters and in October 1957, after his elevation to the cabinet to the chairmanship of an intergovernmental committee of the OEEC, charged with promoting the establishment of a Free Trade Area. During the long and ultimately abortive negotiations that followed, it became clear both that the French objections were not confined to agricultural issues and that there were, and quite rightly, doubts as to Britain's general willingness to accept the merger of sovereignty which was the key to what the architects of the Communities had in mind. By November 1958, the project had to be abandoned. A year later the creation of the European Free Trade Area limited to countries outside the Communities came into being as a result largely of the British initiative.[30]

The question as to whether Britain should swallow its objections and itself apply for membership of the EEC was now an open one. Maudling's experiences had confirmed him in his view that the objections still held. In a speech in the House of Commons on 12 February 1959, he set out what he saw as the heart of the matter:

> we must recognise that to sign the Treaty of Rome would mean having common external tariffs which in turn would mean the end of Commonwealth free entry, and I cannot conceive of any government of this country that would put forward a proposition which involved the abandonment of free entry. It would be wrong for us and for the whole free world to adopt a policy of new duties on foodstuffs and raw materials many of which come from under-developed countries at present entering a major market duty free.[31]

Another sceptic was R. A. Butler, the home secretary, who was aware of the opposition to the idea among the farming community and in his own constituency party.[32] In the end both Maudling and Butler were to go along with Macmillan's attempt to join the EEC, the latter becoming for the period October 1961 to March 1962 the minister in charge of overseeing the negotiations.

It was the evidence that the Six were not prepared for any dilution of their Community into a wider partnership and the unexpectedly rapid development of their discriminatory tariff arrangements that must be held accountable for the fact that joining the EEC, a matter not even mentioned in the Conservative manifesto in the general election of October 1959, became within less than a year a policy to which not only Macmillan but in the end all his colleagues assented. It has been suggested that the turning point for Macmillan was the report of 22 April 1960 of an interdepartmental committee presided over by Sir Frank Lee, recently translated from the Board of Trade to the Treasury. The report pointed out the difficulties that British trade would face if the division of Europe into trading blocs continued. The EFTA Seven were to be a balance for the Six:

> The conclusion is inescapable – that even if one can leave the political factors on one side, from an economic standpoint we must maintain our broad objective of having the UK form part of a single European market unless a still wider grouping, say an Atlantic Free Trade Area – became a possibility.[33]

After a meeting of the Cabinet's European Association Committee on 27 May, Macmillan circulated questions about the future of the Community and about 'the broad political and economic considerations which should determine the choice of policy' and this produced a report presented by the cabinet secretary, Sir Norman Brook, on 6 July.[34]

Most of the report covered familiar ground, giving weight to the economic arguments, to Commonwealth issues and to general questions of foreign policy. One section was specifically devoted to 'sovereignty questions'. It was accepted that there would over the next decade be 'some progressive loss of sovereignty over a number of matters affecting domestic policy of which agriculture was likely to be an important example'. It pointed out that in many cases the precise implications of the terms of the Treaty of Rome had yet to be settled between the Six. By joining the EEC at an early date Britain could take part in such decisions.

> The effects of any eventual loss of sovereignty would be mitigated:
>   1) by our participation in majority voting in the Council of Ministers and by our being able to influence the

Commission's work:
   2) if resistance to Federalism on the part of some of the Governments continues which our membership might be expected to encourage.

Which governments these were who were thought to be resisting federalism is unclear; but in any event, it does appear that some thought had been given to these issues within the Whitehall machine.

On the other hand, the sense that the process in the Community was being understood is diminished by the much greater space devoted to answering under the 'sovereignty' heading the question to what extent Britain's joining the Six would limit its freedom to act independently in matters of foreign policy including external commercial and financial policy. The report agrees that while there is already a measure of interdependence through the Commonwealth relationship and existing alliances as well as the country's own economic weakness such 'interdependence places no constitutional brake on our power of independent decision nor does it call into question our status as a sovereign nation with an identity of our own'. It adds 'if we were to join the Community we would accept treaty limitations on our sovereign of a more precise and definite character than any existing alliances impose'. Since what that would mean in practice would depend upon the evolution of the Community itself, the precise consequences could not easily be foretold.

While Macmillan may only later have reached the definite decision that negotiations for accession should begin, there were indications after the receipt of the Brook report that his mind was moving in that direction. It was the crucial importance of Britain's export trade that he saw as being neglected by those who thought the status quo could be preserved.[35]

While economic considerations seem to have been uppermost in Macmillan's mind, the period when he was moving towards the decision to apply for membership was also one in which other events on the world stage called for attention.

The shift from the Fourth Republic in France to rule by General de Gaulle meant that new elements came into play. Macmillan had achieved in 1958 a bridging of the gap between Britain's nuclear ambitions and the reservations of the United States over the sharing of the technology. But de Gaulle was also determined to see his country as a nuclear power on an equality with the other two western powers and in August 1958 made his suggestion of a virtual triumvirate of the three governments. Since this at once proved unacceptable to the United States and Britain, de Gaulle decided to seek for a closer relationship with Germany as a balance to the Anglo-Saxon world, taking advantage of the simmering problem of Berlin to emphasise France's reliability. Macmillan, while not wholly aware of the intricacies of the Franco-German collusion, did his best to improve relations with de Gaulle in the hope of smoothing Britain's path into Europe.[36]

A change so momentous as would have been the result of EEC membership obviously demanded more than the new outlook of the Prime Minister and his immediate colleagues. But the major domestic and international problems of the period after Macmillan's personal decision to go ahead tended to mask the importance of the issue. Macmillan was able to gain the almost complete support of his party in Parliament in the summer of 1961 for the principle of the application and that of the Party Conference on 12 September. Few significant figures in Conservative politics registered dissent; nor did either the application itself or the de Gaulle veto play any part in the events that led to the resignation of Macmillan and the emergence of his successor Sir Alec Douglas-Home (as Lord Home became) or in the general election of 1964. In so far as Conservative anxieties were expressed they were largely those concerned with the impact of such a change on Britain's relations with the Commonwealth which for a variety of reasons were also under considerable strain at this time.[37]

What is more significant for the remainder of the decade was the fact that the election of 1964 saw the return of a Labour government, some of whose members had served in the Attlee government that had held aloof from the first essay at European integration. Some historians, particularly those sympathetic to the attitude of the original Six in which countries 'Europe' was a cause dear to the entire central element in their politics, irrespective of party, with dissent confined to the two extremes, have blamed Macmillan for not trying to bring about bipartisan support for his application. It could indeed be argued that on practical grounds, the fact that only one of the main parties supported the application and that it would be vulnerable to a change in electoral fortunes might have weakened Britain's negotiating hand. But since the issue was settled on grounds that had little to do with the formal negotiation, the argument would not be a powerful one. In any event the fact is that Macmillan's decision not to seek Labour Party support was a conscious one and due at least in part to his poor opinion of the Labour leader, Hugh Gaitskell.[38]

The actual negotiation of the first attempt to enter the Communities was a dual affair. There were the detailed negotiations at Brussels with the officials about the necessary transitional stage and the political talks in the principal capitals which would determine whether the existing Six would accept Britain's membership.[39] Here de Gaulle's likely attitude was the determining factor. Once again there was the question of whether his political objectives could best be attained by closer ties with Germany. The new Berlin crisis of October 1961 helped to cement the de Gaulle–Adenauer axis, just as it led to closer relations between the British and American governments.[40]

The policy position of the Americans during these Kennedy years were not always consistent. While, as has been seen, their earlier stance had been in favour of European integration, they now entertained worries lest an amalgamation of the two European trading blocs might result in discrimination against their own exports. On the nuclear side, Kennedy seemed favourable to assisting Britain while the Europhiles in the State Department wished to see a downgrading of the 'special relationship' and a single policy towards western Europe taken as a whole.[41] The cancellation of the Skybolt missile on which Britain's hopes for its own deterrent had been based looked like bringing about a crisis in Anglo-American affairs. It was resolved by the decision at the Nassau meeting between Macmillan and Kennedy in December 1962 to allow Britain to acquire the Polaris missile.

For de Gaulle a Britain now closely tied in with the United States in defence matters was an unsuitable partner in the building of Europe. It was believed in some French quarters, though not accepted by the British, that in June 1962 Macmillan had offered France collaboration on nuclear matters in return for supporting the British application at Brussels.[42] And while Adenauer did not share de Gaulle's anti-Americanism he was prepared to see France as an adjunct to his policy of restoring Germany's position. The result was the bilateral Franco-German accord of 22 January 1963 and this gave the signal for de Gaulle's veto of British membership announced by him one week later.[43]

From the point of view of the present inquiry, the most significant fact about the discussions, both public and private, on Britain's application to join the EEC was the lack of importance attached to the issue of sovereignty. The arguments revolved around the likely impact upon the Commonwealth if Britain abandoned a system of preferences and upon agriculture which was intensified by the early acceleration given by the Community to the establishment of its Common Agricultural Policy. The latter was connected with another issue that received attention, the way in which the levies collected on agricultural imports would be divided between the member countries. It was almost as though the government and its advisers could not bring themselves to take seriously the institutional provisions of the Treaty of Rome, let alone the conviction of their creators that this was to be a foundation for further integration, a springboard for further development towards a United States of Europe.

Only a handful of Conservative dissidents raised the question of the passage of law-making powers to the Community or the priority which such legislation would have over the enactments of the United Kingdom Parliament.

In so far as Macmillan was aware of doubts on this score, his reaction was not to investigate them in a direct fashion but to rely on the by now committed views of the Foreign Office and its representatives abroad to provide ammunition by which such doubts could be stilled. He thus in June 1961 instructed the Foreign Office to issue a questionnaire to the British Ambassadors in all the EEC countries by which they were to ascertain how far the Community had impinged upon the 'attributions' of the national parliaments and how the parliaments reacted to Community legislation which ran counter to national legislation or national practices. They were also to ask whether the EEC itself was gaining or losing in popularity in the country concerned.[44]

Needless to say all the replies were thoroughly reassuring. No difficulties of the kind referred to had become evident and membership of the Community was generally welcome. Indeed the occasion was taken, notably by Sir Pierson Dixon, the ambassador in Paris and a convinced Euro-enthusiast, to stress the advantages that would follow from Britain's entry into the Community. The questions asked were obviously unreal. The Community's legislative and judicial powers were new and untried and in June 1961, at the height of the Khrushchev–Kennedy confrontation, most Europeans had other things on their mind. As indeed did Macmillan, who announced his decision to apply for membership on 31 July. In a debate in the House of Lords on 2 August, Lord Home played down the political aspect of the decision to seek accession by declaring that the 'surrender of sovereignty is restricted to economic matters'.[45]

Although there had been Euro-enthusiasts within the Labour Party, particularly among those who had contacts with socialist parties in western Europe, there had been little disposition when the party entered its long period in opposition in 1951 to reverse the policy of aloofness from integrationist moves adopted by the Attlee government. In so far as it looked beyond domestic matters, it was more concerned to accelerate the process of decolonisation and to

see the Commonwealth develop into a multi-ethnic grouping. It had a large component hostile to nuclear weapons.
Many of its members were also on the lookout for opportunities to minimise confrontation with the Soviet Union
and to restore by so doing the original concept of the United
Nations. The Right–Left division which became more obvious after Attlee's restraining hand was removed was not
originally one over 'Europe'.

The struggle for the leadership as Attlee's departure
approached was settled by Gaitskell's determination to prevent the party from electing Aneurin Bevan and coming
under the domination of the Left.[46] On Europe, Gaitskell
was an agnostic, sympathising neither with those who were
strong opponents nor, like Roy Jenkins, strong supporters.
He did not think the issue one of principle; Britain while
obviously having an interest in Europe had strong ties with
the Commonwealth and the United States which made
'going into a federation of Europe out of the question'. For
economic advance Britain must look primarily to its own
efforts.[47]

Despite his public pronouncements, close colleagues believed that Gaitskell was at heart in favour of membership
of the EEC but accepted his view that to announce a
decision either way would create public divisions within the
party which could be turned to the Conservatives' advantage. That position was maintained after Macmillan opened
negotiations for entry in July 1962, though in private
Gaitskell conceded that, if given acceptable terms, membership might be an advantage in preventing the Community
developing in ways inimical to a wider view of the world's
needs.

The decision to enter into negotiations came as something
of a surprise to the Labour leadership. At the conclusion
of the House of Lords debate on 2 August 1961, Attlee led
the Labour peers in abstaining. The course of the negotiations between that date and de Gaulle's veto were closely
followed by the Labour leadership with the object of finding a policy on which the party could unite since there
were in the leadership and in the rank and file adherents of

both a pro-European and an anti-European stance. Some of the leading figures were engaged in pro-market campaigning while there were radical opponents whom Gaitskell described on the radio in October 1961 as a coalition between a Little England Right and a frequently pro-Russian Left.[48]

Gaitskell's own views were still unfixed. It was certainly his intention to probe the attitudes of the other countries involved as to the possibility of some looser and broader association which would enable Britain's Commonwealth ties to be retained. In April 1962, Gaitskell, together with his economic experts, met with Jean Monnet on the initiative of Roy Jenkins. He found Monnet unwilling to enter into Britain's particular problems and evasive on the likely impact of the EEC upon Third World countries.[49]

When the terms reached by Heath were made public, Gaitskell felt that he had been deceived and that Heath had given way on the vital issues.[50] In particular he saw the Common Agricultural Policy with its implications for Commonwealth trade wholly unacceptable. It seemed impossible to separate terms that were unacceptable from opposition to entry in principle and it was therefore the latter that appeared to be the message of his television address on 21 September 1962 when he asked whether Macmillan's claim that Britain should join a larger group of nations meant the end of Britain as an independent nation. If so, 'we become no more than "Texas" or "California" in the United States of Europe. It means the end of a thousand years of history'.[51] Gaitskell's move towards a hostile interpretation of the proposed British membership was completed in the speech he gave to the Labour Party Conference at Brighton on 3 October. The economic arguments for it were weak, the political dangers of becoming a 'province of Europe' unacceptable. That after all was what was meant by 'federation', which was what the creators of the Community were openly seeking.[52]

In October Gaitskell, deciding that a mere negative stance was insufficient, asked Harold Wilson to organise a committee including Denis Healey, James Callaghan, Douglas Jay and Peter Shore to look to formulate a policy on which the party might unite. The committee accepted the substance of a memorandum from one of Gaitskell's associates, John Murray, who had come round from a strong pro-European position in 1957 to questioning the basis of the EEC. The memorandum was not made public but a summary was published in 1995. While much of the memorandum reiterated the usual arguments about the alleged economic advantages of entry and the baneful impact it would have on the Commonwealth, one paragraph in the summary is worth giving in full:

> The political objectives of the EEC were dangerously obscure, any suggestion of submerging our sovereign ability to determine our own essential affairs in some larger European entity would be anathema to most British people, who were all too well aware of the collectivist and, worse, political tendencies of some of our proposed partners. Since Article 145 of the Treaty of Rome conferred administrative powers on the Commission, who were in turn responsible to an *ad hoc* Council of Ministers who had powers to take decisions over which the Court of Justice had rights of enforcement, there was *prima facie* a very serious erosion of sovereignty involved; not the limited concessions made through clearly defined specific arrangements but a general derogation of power. The Government did not seem to have been very zealous in trying to clarify this question. Were we giving away our political birthright under the guise of a trading relationship. And if there was no question of political union as we were repeatedly assured there was not why not just have a trading relationship?[53]

It is clear that Gaitskell himself subscribed to these doubts. His premature death put the question of Labour policy once more into the melting-pot. Of the committee, Jay and Shore remained constant in their doubts about the EEC; Wilson, Callaghan and Healey were to become to different degrees partisans of British membership.

How Gaitskell's own determination in his last months to campaign against the British entry into the EEC would have survived the changes brought about by de Gaulle's veto it is not possible to say. Clearly he now found himself with strange allies. It had been Douglas Jay's hope that the unanswerable case made by Gaitskell, particularly on the political implications of entry, would settle the matter not only for the Labour Party but for the country and for the rest of the century.[54]

During the interval between de Gaulle's veto and the end of the period of Conservative rule in 1964, the Conservatives, first under Macmillan and then under Sir Alec Douglas-Home, were too preoccupied with other issues, both domestic and international, for any change to be made in its general pro-European commitment. The increasing implausibility of the Commonwealth as an alternative agent of British influence weakened the position of the anti-Europeans in the Conservative Party who saw themselves reduced to an unfashionable fringe. When Gaitskell's successor, Harold Wilson, took office in 1964, he was seen as an anti-marketeer supporting Gaitskell in 1961–2 against many of Gaitskell's friends. But his cabinet was largely dominated by prominent pro-marketeers such as Roy Jenkins, Tony Benn and George Brown. And when the election of 1966 gave him a comfortable majority he felt able to go on a pilgrimage with George Brown to the capitals of Europe, seeking for encouragement for Britain to enter the Communities on terms he could persuade his party to accept. With the opposition now led by Ted Heath there was nothing to fear from that quarter.[55]

It is difficult to know on what grounds Wilson himself based his change of stance. There is no indication that he ever analysed the nature of the EEC or what membership would mean.[56] It is perhaps safest to say that by now the British intellectual scene and above all sentiment in Whitehall had become imbued with the pro-European bias that was to be there during the next quarter of a century.

The porousness of the discussions in Wilson's cabinet made the shifting of opinion in 1966–7 fairly easy to follow.

The subsequent publication of the diaries of cabinet members illustrates the process by which even reluctant colleagues were brought along. Richard Crossman recorded on 10 September 1966 that the Commonwealth was 'fading out as an organisation' and that this would suggest entry into the EEC. On 13 September he recorded his view that if it were possible to enter the EEC that year one should not turn it down straightaway: 'I haven't found the twenty months we have spent outside Europe and close to America very attractive, particularly in view of our new subordinate relation to President Johnson.'[57]

On 22 October the cabinet met at Chequers for a long meeting with officials and advisers and Crossman found Stewart and Brown committed to entry. The questions raised were economic. Would the abolition of exchange controls mean an immediate devaluation and was membership of the Community compatible with socialist planning at home? Crossman believed the agricultural aspect pushed by Jay and the agriculture minister Fred Peart was secondary as in a period of growth the price rises could be sustained. The splits in the cabinet were clearly set out. Again the question was discussed at a cabinet meeting on 1 November and again on 3 November by which time the cabinet was clearly coming round to letting Wilson and Brown go on their tour with an announced intention to seek membership if the terms were acceptable. Crossman at a meeting on 7 November pressed Wilson to take the matter into his own hands. At a cabinet meeting on 9 November Crossman said he was himself a 'little Englander' but felt it was not a position which would be found generally acceptable until 'Europe' had been tried and found to be impossible.[58]

The Wilson–Brown tour of the European capitals early in 1967 left them with the conviction that they could have entry; though when they reported to the cabinet it was suggested that they had given a misleading picture of the extent to which de Gaulle had come round to accept the idea of Britain's entry. In the cabinet only Jay was now totally against entry. By the time the cabinet met for yet another discussion on 6 April, Wilson was clearly wholly

committed to a pro-market view.[59] At a meeting in 20 April
the cabinet's papers included a note from Sir Burke Trend
representing the views of all the permanent secretaries to the
effect that there was no future whatsoever for a Britain that
failed to get into the Community.[60] The question of whether
what happened to British opinion would explain Wilson's
change of attitude was asked even by those who took an
active part in the debates of the time:

Douglas Jay in a book published in 1980 well after British
membership was an accomplished fact put the question:

> why did almost the whole British establishment – the
> government machine, the City and the press – and only
> during the 1960s turn a simultaneous somersault, and
> embrace a policy which was bound to burden heavily our
> balance of payments, lower our living standards, weaken
> our international influence, alienate our best friends over-
> seas and damage the control of our own Parliament over
> our own affairs?[61]

Douglas Jay suggests various reasons why elements in
support of the Conservative Party were attracted by what
they thought participation in the EEC might bring. But
these arguments had no doubt been taken into account by
Macmillan. What needs explaining is the abandonment by
most of the Labour Party of Gaitskell's position at a time
when the arguments that prevailed with Labour in the late
1980s and the 1990s – greater socialist-style interventionism
in the economy and in Labour relations – were not present
since on the whole the dominant strands in European
politics in the mid-1960s were of a rightish complexion. For
while it is true that the 'European movement' was spending
a great deal of money in propaganda, much of it was not of
a kind that would directly influence the Labour Party or its
trade union backers.

It is tempting to look at personalities in the government
and their sources of advice. When Wilson was forced to
abandon his first choice as foreign secretary, Patrick Gordon-Walker, because of his failure to secure a seat in the
new Parliament, he turned to Michael Stewart.[62] He was in

Jay's view converted to a pro-EEC position by Con O'Neill who returned to the Foreign Office in 1965 after serving as ambassador to the EEC. The pro-EEC briefing he produced in 1966 led also to the setting-up of a 'European Integration Unit' in the Foreign Office and henceforward the Foreign Office identified its own interests with those of British membership as future foreign secretaries were to discover.

The pro-Community (later pro-Union) stance has remained a feature of the Foreign and Commonwealth Office thinking and of the outlook of the holders of Britain's major embassies abroad. In retirement in the House of Lords and elsewhere such individuals became vehicles for pro-Union propaganda, helping thereby in shaping media reaction and so public opinion at large.

By the time Britain's membership was confirmed in the referendum of 1975, this position was an entrenched one as successive secretaries of state were bound to discover.

The FCO was prepared to see some faults in the EEC, but it retained the evangelist's faith: when Callaghan had gone to meetings and was even mildly critical of the EEC the media were not discouraged from describing him as 'crass'.[63] His successor Crosland was to encounter the same set of convictions as did Crosland's own successor David Owen.

> the biggest source of friction I had to contend with at the Foreign Office was a relatively small number of senior diplomats who had been used to having a campaigning role over the European Community and had built up strong links with journalists sympathetic to Europe . . . Some of them had become zealots for the European Community and all its works and were none too keen to accept political control. In particular they found it hard to understand that my determination to spill a little blood on the diplomatic carpets of Europe from time to time was not playing to anti-European sentiment, but stemmed from the belief that having a sticking point and being prepared to stand one's ground upon occasion was necessary to protect British interests. They also did not

comprehend that my distaste and disdain for moves
deigned to pave the way for the Euro-federalists dream,
the United States of Europe was all of a piece with my
long standing and strong commitment to Britain's playing
a full part in the European Community.[64]

The question raised by Lord Owen's account is whether
these British civil servants were instrumental in hiding from
their political masters the fact which was evident enough by
the time Lord Owen's memoirs were published, that the
Euro-federalists' dream was not something added on to the
idea of the Community but was at the very heart of the
objectives of its most determined continental advocates.

A meeting at Chequers on 30 April revealed doubts about
the likelihood of economic benefits in the early years of
membership, but those who had in Crossman's view abandoned the idea of a socialist planned economy – Stewart,
Brown, Wilson and Callaghan – were keen on using entry
in order to secure the abandonment of that commitment.[65]
It is obvious that members of the cabinet at this juncture
were hard to divide into pro- and anti-marketeers. On 1
May, Crossman decries a list produced in that morning's
Guardian and gives one of his own under the headings 'Yes,
without qualification', 'No without qualification' and
'Maybe'. Crossman lists not only himself among the last
category but also Stewart who two days earlier he had put
among the whole-hearted advocates of entry.[66] Gordon-Walker's diary gives a different division with 13 favouring entry,
six a declaration of principle and two being opposed.[67]

Such differences of opinion about where individuals stood
on the issue must make one wonder at the degree to which
the whole matter was being seen in the round rather than
subordinated to other considerations of party policy and
party management. It is clear that the basic constitutional
issue was hardly faced and that few members of the government now took account of the degree to which those
governing the affairs of the Community in Europe were
devoted to a federal solution to Europe's problems or were
ready to accept a Britain clearly reluctant to endorse it.

The first draft of a paper submitted to cabinet on 3 July was 'political', even touching on defence to a degree worrying to some members, but the redraft was allowed to go through.[68] When the declaration was presented to the Party Conference on 5 October, the government line was supported by a two-to-one majority. Nevertheless, its policy was unsustainable. Shortly afterwards the EEC Commission issued a statement to the effect that Britain's economy was too weak for her to be allowed to join, and on 27 November, de Gaulle produced his second veto.

The Conservative victory in the general election of 1970 brought Heath into power as Prime Minister. His freedom to pursue his European inclinations was enhanced by the fact that France was no longer ruled by de Gaulle and that his more pragmatic successor, Georges Pompidou, was in the end prepared to accept British membership of the EEC. What was of equal significance was that the Community itself had been further consolidated, with the Common Agricultural Policy in particular having received its definitive shape in 1969. Although it has been claimed that some successes were achieved by Britain's negotiators who began their task in October 1970, it has also been argued that it was only a direct approach by Heath to Pompidou that clinched the matter. Once again verbal ambiguities were helpful, Pompidou assuring British viewers on television that by 'Europe' he did not mean 'federalism'. France and Britain shared a common approach to integration and both wished to preserve their national identities.[69]

Agreement was reached in June and the terms published in a White Paper in July. The White Paper was discussed by the cabinet and seems to have been regarded as acceptable. It was only later that serious Conservative misgivings began to be voiced. As a junior member of the cabinet was to write many years later, paragraphs 29–32 dealing with the constitutional aspects of the agreement 'stand out as an extraordinary example of artful confusion to conceal fundamental issues'.[70] Lady Thatcher calls attention to two sentences in particular: 'There is no question of any erosion of national sovereignty; what is proposed is a sharing and enlargement of individual sovereignties in the general interest'; and 'The common law will remain the basis of our legal system, and our Courts will continue to operate as they do at present.'

Since the Labour Party was clearly divided, it was on the reactions of the Conservative Party in the country and in Parliament that the issue of putting the agreement into effect now depended.

On 14 July Heath addressed the Conservative Central Council and received an overwhelming measure of support. At the Party Conference in the autumn a pro-EEC motion was carried by 2474 to 324. The parliamentary arithmetic was less certain, with some thirty Conservatives still opposed to entry, mainly on the issue of sovereignty. Heath was persuaded by his senior colleagues not to try to force the issue through by exerting the full powers of the whips but to put the issue to a free vote of the House of Commons and rely on the divisions in the Labour Party to achieve the necessary majority.[71]

Wilson would have been ready to agree to a free vote but was not backed by the anti-marketeers in his shadow cabinet, fortified by the majority against entry at the party's special conference in July and at the annual conference in October.[72] By this time the anti-marketeers had received a new and important recruit in Tony Benn who had changed sides on the issue.[73] The Parliamentary Party voted by 140 to 111 against permitting a free vote, so the whips were on to vote against the government motion, and the pro-market front-bench spokesmen, Roy Jenkins, George Thomson and Harold Lever, were debarred from taking part in the six-day debate which opened on 21 October. The debate in which 176 MPs spoke ended on 28 October with a vote of 356 to 244, a government majority of 112. Sixty-nine Labour members had defied their whip and voted for entry and another 20 had abstained. Thirty-nine Conservatives voted against; two abstained and another was absent ill. In the Lords the government majority was overwhelming, 451 to 58.

To make these votes effective, it was still necessary to give legislative effect to the decision and this was done in the European Communities Bill, a short bill of only 12 clauses and 4 schedules of which the heart was in Clause II which provided that EEC law should prevail over British law and be 'enforced, allowed and followed accordingly'. The opposition with few exceptions was prepared to fight the bill, clause by clause, and at times during its passage, majorities were very narrow with some dissident Tories ready to go into the opposition lobby. Clause II was only carried by 8 votes thanks to Liberal support and Labour abstentions. But in the end the third reading was carried by 301 to 284. Royal assent came on 17 October and on 1 January 1973 Britain became a member of the EEC.[74]

The question was whether this decision was a commitment for ever. In the debate on Clause II, Geoffrey Howe, the solicitor-general who had had an important hand in framing the bill, gave an assurance that if total repeal was ever suggested, 'the ultimate sovereignty of Parliament must remain intact'. But going on to what exactly would happen if future Acts of Parliament conflicted with Community law he said that 'the Courts would . . . in accordance with the traditional approach interpret statute in accordance with our international obligations'. If these could not be matched, one could not do more than that 'to reconcile the inescapable and enduring sovereignty of Parliament at the end of the road with the proposition that we should give effect to our Treaty obligations to provide for the precedence of Community Law. If through inadvertence any such conflict arose, that would be a matter for consideration by the government of the day'.[75]

Meanwhile the process of integration was not slowing down. In October 1973, Heath attended a summit of the Community leaders in Paris at which they agreed that economic and monetary union should be achieved by 1980.[76]

The problems that led to the election of February 1974 and the fall of the Heath government were not connected with the European issue, nor did that issue figure largely in the election though Enoch Powell's raising of it in the last few days of the campaign and his revelation that it had led him to cast a postal vote for Labour made some impact.[77]

The Labour victory was consolidated by the second election, in October, in which again the European question was not to the fore. By then it was clear that whatever Powell may have thought earlier, the Wilson–Callaghan leadership of the Labour Party was intent on keeping British membership in being.

The difficulty for Wilson was the fact that divisions over Europe still ran deep in the Labour Party. When in March 1972, the Labour shadow cabinet had supported an amendment to make British entry conditional on a referendum, Roy Jenkins, Harold Lever and George Thomson had resigned, although they drifted back over the succeeding years.[78] Edmund Dell had resigned after the vote on 28 October 1979 when he was among those who had defied the party whip in order to vote for entry.[79] At the 1973 Party Conference, Wilson secured agreement for a policy of renegotiating membership to be followed by a referendum on the terms obtained.[80] And this policy figured in the Labour manifesto at both the February and October 1974 general elections.

It was a policy of calculated ambiguity: the two sections of the warring party did not mean the same thing by renegotiations. 'The opponents of membership wanted to negotiate for a breakdown by attempting to secure terms which the rest of the Community could not possibly accept. Supporters of membership accepted that there was a limit to the concessions that the other member states could then be expected to make.'[81]

The terms for renegotiation were agreed by the cabinet of 7 March 1974 and discussions in the cabinet subsequently revealed the depth of disagreement.[82] As one of the chief anti-marketeers put it in her diary on 7 November: 'I personally believe that we are being inched into the market by a succession of small faits accomplis and that the Commonwealth is dying the death by a thousand scratches.'[83]

The negotiations were largely left to Callaghan who toured Europe to see what could be achieved.[84] But the intention to succeed robbed them of reality. Roy Jenkins's later verdict that 'the whole exercise had more of cosmetics than of reality about it' is hard to dispute.[85]

It may be that the team set up by Wilson to oversee the negotiations slipped from an anti-market to a pro-market stance.[86] In fact, given the extent to which the integration of the Community had proceeded, there was little that could be done on the issues – Commonwealth sugar for instance – that most worried some cabinet members. The main issue and one that was not to vanish was the extent of Britain's contribution to the Community budget in the light of her position as a prime importer of the commodities upon which a levy had to be paid. The issue was discussed *inter alia* when the heads of the now Nine EEC countries met at Paris on 9 and 10 December.[87] At this meeting agreement on a financial formula was reached and Wilson also accepted the principle of direct elections for the European Parliament for which the cabinet had never given a mandate. Although the negotiations were still in progress it was clear that Wilson would recommend their outcome despite misgivings in the cabinet when he reported on 12 December. He brushed aside the point that the communiqué had declared the heads of government to be still committed to economic and monetary union.[88]

Benn in an open letter to his constituents revealed the depth of opposition to the terms agreed: 'Britain's continuing membership of the Community would mean the end of Britain as a completely self-governing nation and the end of our democratically elected Parliament as the supreme law-making body of the United Kingdom.'[89] The solution for this divergence was the cabinet decision on 21 January 1975 that the terms for staying in would be put to the nation in a referendum with cabinet members being free to campaign either way.

On March 10–11 a final stage of the negotiations took place in Dublin and Wilson felt able to announce in the House of Commons on March 18 that the terms there were satisfactory and that the government would recommend their acceptance. After a debate in the House of Commons on 7, 8 and 9 April, the terms were approved but with 144

Labour members voting against the motion. A special Labour Party Conference on 26 April came out against the terms but, with some disregard for the party's constitution, the party machine was instructed by the National Executive Committee to remain neutral in the coming referendum campaign.[90]

Meanwhile the cabinet itself returned to the subject from time to time. The most far-reaching discussion took place on 18 March when according to Benn's account 'for the first time the question of sovereignty was discussed properly'. While he had some support, other ministers dismissed as academic the question of whether the Community was to be a supranational structure or a community of sovereign states. The Lord Chancellor sought to dismiss the sovereignty argument by pointing out that Parliament would still have the right to repudiate the treaty at any time.[91] While it is clear that Parliament could repeal the European Communities Act, how it would go about freeing Britain from the constraints of a treaty of unlimited duration is not altogether clear.

Since the validity of Britain's continued membership of the Community, and so now of the European Union, is often based on the argument that the British in a free referendum voted themselves in, a leader of the pro-EEC all-party campaign has given a detailed account of his own role.[92] There were in addition party campaigns both pro and anti, and some cross-party collaboration on the anti side. On the Conservative side, the replacement of Edward Heath by Margaret Thatcher as party leader in February freed Heath to play a leading part both in the all-party and the Conservative pro-Europe campaigns.[93] Mrs Thatcher herself while campaigning for a 'yes' vote did so in a fairly minor key.[94]

Lord Callaghan's account suggests that the scales were held even since the 'Government financed the printing and circulation of leaflets to every household, seeking out both the pro-Market and anti-Market case, together with the government's own recommendation' while also providing grants of £125 000 to the two campaigning organisations. Yet he admits that the 'pro-Marketeers held the advantage in money, organization and press sympathy, as well the prestige conveyed by a recommendation from the Government backed by the Conservative and Liberal Parties'.[95]

In fact the scales were more loaded than he suggests. For one thing, just as at the time of Britain's entry, the government's own statement played down the full implications of membership. The officials working upon it, all by now accepting the common Whitehall position of welcoming Britain's membership of the Community, were not prepared to see any material provided that might help the anti-Market campaigners among ministers. An information unit set up by the FCO to deal with inquiries from the public was bound to take a similar line.

Furthermore resources for the two campaigns were by no means balanced. When Lord Callaghan refers to 'money', what he means is that the government's grant to the pro-Market campaign was supplemented by funds from private business and the 'European Movement' on a very considerable scale.[96] And that body as we now know was the beneficiary of much American government largesse.[97]

What is clear is that the protagonists of the case for Britain remaining in the Community never explained that the issue transcended matters of commercial policy, or that while they pointed to Britain's right to pull out if a future Parliament should so decree it was never suggested that what was being embarked upon was a voyage in company with those who saw the achievements of the Community to date as only a stepping stone to 'more perfect union'. As Lord Jay points out: 'No sanction whatever was given in the Referendum for moves towards a Federal EEC or for steps towards Federation such as direct elections to an EEC Assembly or for economic and monetary union.' These did not figure in either the government's own pamphlets or in the propaganda of Roy Jenkins's 'Britain in Europe'. Indeed the government pamphlet, despite the Paris summit, explicitly rejected economic and monetary union.[98] Heath himself had indeed, in the Commons debate on 9 April, insisted that the Community's purpose had all along been political: initially to foster a Franco-German *rapprochement* and contain

Germany within a European framework, and now to build Europe's independent strength alongside the United States and the Soviet Union. This purpose did involve some sacrifice of sovereignty but that, he believed, was fully justified.

Such outspokenness was not characteristic of the referendum campaign in the country where the long-term vision implicit in Heath's position was played down in favour of more mundane arguments. This, says Heath's sympathetic biographer, was 'unquestionably good politics, from the point of view of inducing an insular British electorate to take the plunge, and not necessarily consciously dishonest. Yet there is undoubtedly a case for saying', he admits, 'that Parliament in 1971 and the country in 1975 was hoodwinked into signing up for more than it was ever told.'[99]

A former civil servant involved in the campaign and himself a pro-European has put it even more bluntly: 'the Labour government's referendum of 1975 was a fraud perpetrated by civil servants with the then government's connivance, designed (rightly in my opinion) to keep us in but also (wrongly) to conceal so far as possible the countervailing disadvantages of membership.'[100]

In the light of such comments and of the overwhelming evidence to support them, it is curious to find someone much involved in these events still denying that the British electorate was ever misled on the implications of membership.[101]

In any event the electorate behaved as they were expected to do and on a 65 per cent turn-out decided by a ratio of two to one that Britain should remain in the Community.

5 Europe in British Politics, 1975–91

The referendum of 1975 confirmed Britain's membership of the European Community and for the time being resolved the internal problems of the Labour Party. The domestic problems that confronted first the Wilson and then the Callaghan government made further ventilating of doubts about 'Europe' unacceptable even to those who had not endorsed the arguments in favour of membership.

It had not of course solved the problem of the indifference of British ministers to what was afoot among their new partners as had already been clear when Wilson went along with the communiqué of the Paris summit in October 1973 with its call for a European Union by 1980.

As a former head of the FCO has pointed out,

> Many of the problems which have since dogged the Community already began to appear at this meeting but few in the United Kingdom anticipated how the debate in the Community would develop during the next two decades. Those British who were interested misjudged the extent to which they would be able to shape the development of the Community whilst the 'founding fathers' were careful not to disclose their ultimate federal objectives. History will recall how we were steadily outsmarted between 1972 and 1992.[1]

By now however many British officials had become convinced that, whatever their political masters might believe, Britain had no alternative but to take a full part in the process of European integration and not allow the new institutions to be dominated wholly by a Franco-German combination which seemed particularly close while Helmut Schmidt was German Chancellor and Giscard d'Estaing President of France. Their anxieties became more acute when Callaghan replaced Wilson as Prime Minister in April

85

1976. Nicholas Henderson as ambassador at Bonn had already formed a poor opinion of Callaghan when he visited Bonn soon after he became foreign secretary because of his insularity of approach to the European issues.[2] As ambassador to Paris in 1978, he confirmed his original impression of the then Prime Minister: 'with Schmidt, Giscard feels that he does not have a large anti-European extremist wing of his political party always tugging at him. They obviously get along very well and have complete trust in each other. Callaghan can inspire trust more than did Wilson but he always displays an unequivocally non-continental attitude.' One result in Henderson's view was that the other member states no longer thought Britain could stand up against French nationalism and possible German assertiveness.[3]

Of general questions relating to the development of the Community the most important at that time was the question of entry into the European Monetary System where in Whitehall political arguments in favour of entry and not standing out against the other eight member states were thought to be decisive.[4] Similar questions arose out of the large deficit in Britain's net contribution to the budget.[5] Given the nature of the Community's financial arrangements, this could have been foreseen.

On actual issues in the Community's development, Britain went along with the other member. It took part in the European Monetary System (EMS) when that began to function in 1979 and, after some reluctance in the cabinet, provided for the first direct elections to the European Parliament to be held in the United Kingdom, as elsewhere in Europe.[6]

Although some additional scope was given to the European Parliament in its new shape, it was not to be central to the next phase in the development of the Community. Its importance for British politics was that while those nominated to the Assembly (as the Parliament had hitherto been styled) had been rooted in their parties at home, the new MEPs regarded themselves as having greater independence and greater importance, as indeed their lavish salaries and perquisites might well have suggested. This feeling of independence was enhanced by the fact that the Parliament was organised in terms of party groupings so that the MEPs from one country needed to seek associates elsewhere. With both major British parties divided and with Labour after its 1979 election defeat going through a period of anti-European sentiment under left-wing leadership, the country was for the time being out of step with its continental counterparts.[7] The Conservatives found themselves in an even more difficult position since the British Conservative Party has no exact continental counterparts. Efforts to build bridges with the German CDU and other Christian Democratic parties ran into trouble since 'Christian Democracy' had been and remained an essential element in the continental coalition pressing for more rapid and far-reaching steps towards integration. The result was that by the elections of June 1995 Conservative MEPs were from the European Parliament's point of view members of the 'European People's Party' whose programme was the opposite of the goal of a looser Europe enunciated by the Prime Minister, John Major. At the same time, the Labour Party, having switched under the leadership of John Smith and Tony Blair to a strongly pro-federalist position, had among its representatives a few committed to the earlier sceptical position still upheld domestically by Tony Benn. By a final irony Neil Kinnock, under whose leadership the Labour Party had been committed against membership of the Community in its existing form and whose House of Commons followers had almost succeeded in defeating the Treaty of Maastricht, was now a European commissioner and his wife an MEP.

From the continental point of view it was no doubt a matter for regret that the political forces in Britain most committed to integration, the Liberals and, after their secession from Labour in 1981, the Social Democrats, later to form an alliance with the Liberals and ultimately to be absorbed by them, were, thanks to the operation of the first-past-the-post electoral system, given no representation in the European Parliament at all until 1994.[8]

Such anomalies in respect of the nomenclature and behaviour of political parties are not unique to Britain. Indeed when the British Liberals got to Strasbourg, they found themselves very distant from the Italians or others calling themselves Liberals. British Liberals had now become part of a near-collectivist consensus on the British Left while continental Liberals whose ideological provenance was quite different were still wedded to ideas of *laissez-faire*.

It is natural that countries whose history has been so different, particularly in relation to the advent of democracy, should have quite different party systems. On the other hand, all experience suggests that no parliamentary system can work unless it functions through political parties extending over much of the area it purports to represent.[9] No such parties exist or can be expected to exist in 'Europe' whether of the Six, the Twelve, the Fifteen or whatever number of countries may eventually enter the Union if it survives. All attempts to upgrade the role of the Parliament are bound to collapse on that vital obstacle.

While statesmen seriously concerned to push forward the policies of the Community might pay lip-service to the notion of enhancing the powers of the Parliament as a way of handling the 'democratic deficit', they were, unless the prisoners of ideology, well aware both of the degree of irresponsibility shown by many of its members and of the fact that the 'Euro-elections' themselves did not for the most part reflect a sounding of opinion on European issues. It was fairly obvious that in most if not all countries, these elections came to be seen as corresponding to opinion polls testing the popularity or lack of it of incumbent governments.

On the other hand, the same statesmen were well aware of the possible impact of national elections upon the fortunes of the Community with decisions on major matters often being either hastened or delayed by speculating upon their outcome. Since the ministers representing national governments formed the Community's legislature, their individual political complexion was obviously very important. The situation was different from that in most federations where elections to the federal executive and or legislature are separate in time from elections in the units of which the federation is composed. As already pointed out, the only exception is provided by Germany where the composition of the Upper House – the Bundesrat – depends on the outcome of elections in the *Länder* which, like elections in the states of the European Union, are not held at any one time.

Had British Liberal Democrats, as the Liberals called themselves after swallowing up the Social Democrats, taken an objective view of the way in which to hurry on the creation of a United States of Europe, they would have emphasised the need to have all national elections in Europe on a single timetable rather than pursue their party ends by seeking to get Britain to introduce proportional representation for elections to the European Parliament: Britain had been committed to a uniform electoral procedure across the Community since 1976.

In any event, when the Conservatives returned to power in 1979 the commitment to direct elections was in existence and there was through the Committee of Permanent Representatives an increasing involvement of Whitehall officialdom with the framing of Community policies. The fact that Britain's membership of the EMS had not included participation in the Exchange Rate Mechanism – the ERM – presented the incoming government with a problem which was to worry it for the whole of its life.[10]

Europe did not figure strongly among the early preoccupations of the Thatcher government which had to deal with the Labour government's legacy of industrial unrest and economic profligacy. Mrs Thatcher herself, although a member of Heath's cabinet at the time of Britain's entry into the Community and supporting the majority party line in the referendum, was no enthusiast for the European ideology and more concerned to build good relations with the United States, a determination amply repaid by the invaluable support received from the United States at the time of the Falklands War.[11] As someone of a younger generation than Heath, that is, too young to have had an active role in the Second World War but not young enough to regard it as past history, she tended to look with suspicion at what could appear to be a vehicle for German aggrandisement. Her main interests were in domestic politics – the rolling-back of what she saw as the postwar collectivist consensus and the changes made in successive stages in the composition of her cabinet reflected this priority rather than greater or lesser degrees of commitment to the European vision.

In the first years of the new administration European issues could fairly safely be put on the back burner. Indeed the protagonists of European integration are prone to regard the period following the enlargement of membership in the early 1970s as one of relative stagnation in the Community's history. What changed matters was the advent in January 1985 to the presidency of the Commission of the French socialist politician, Jacques Delors, who was close to the socialist President of France, François Mitterrand, who had replaced Giscard d'Estaing in May 1981, and who, having abandoned the left-wing policies of the first couple of years of his presidency, was prepared to seek new laurels on the international scene.[12] A third new presence on the scene was the German Chancellor, Helmut Kohl, who had replaced Schmidt in October 1982. While his own commitment to out-and-out European federalism has sometimes been questioned, his party, the CDU, was strongly imbued with the views and doctrines that had led Adenauer to adopt this route during Germany's period of weakness after the war. It was now to be a vehicle of Germany's new strength based upon economic growth and relatively limited commitment to defence and overseas expenditure.[13]

While it would be wrong to see these three powerful personalities as some kind of troika, since each had a different agenda and a different set of priorities, they did intend in their different ways to end the period of relative quiescence in the affairs of the Community and to contribute to the removal of what they saw as the outstanding obstacles to the pursuit of its original goals, that is, a return to positions originally expressed in various declarations of principle – completion of a single market involving all aspects of economic policy, common social policies partly for their own sake and partly to ensure that the burdens they imposed upon economic activity were evenly spread, and a common attitude and negotiating stance towards the rest of the world. While in the early years this had meant claiming for 'Europe' parity with the superpowers, the United States and the Soviet Union, by the late 1980s, there was consciousness of another looming threat, the burgeoning economies of the Pacific rim and ultimately of China.[14]

If these goals were to be taken seriously it was hard to see how a clash with Britain could be avoided, unless Britain was brought round to adopting similar attitudes and similar principles. From the beginning in 1950 until the last years of the socialist governments of the 1970s, Britain had constantly opposed the surrender of elements of national sovereignty, and even when they had effectively been abandoned, had placed emphasis on each member's right of veto to limit further advance towards a full federal system. As was seen in an earlier chapter, the ceaseless activity of the Court did push further the bounds within which Community action appeared to be confined by the Treaty of Rome but this was itself inadequate for the purposes of the true believers. Institutional change was also required both to minimise the exercise of any national veto and formally to extend the range of the Community's powers. The period of Margaret Thatcher's government and the early part of the premiership of her successor John Major thus were in retrospect primarily concerned with the negotiation and implementation of two major European agreements, the Single European Act and the Treaty of European Union, the Treaty of Maastricht. Yet to anyone following the course of events from year to year and summit to summit, two other matters, a hangover from earlier disputes, bulk as large or even larger, the question of Britain's net contribution to the Community budget and its entry into and departure from the ERM.

In the course of all these sets of overlapping and at times interlocking negotiations, there are signs that within government itself major differences over policy as well as tactics were emerging. Margaret Thatcher's premiership was brought to an end because her differences over 'Europe' with her chancellor of the exchequer and her foreign secretary persuaded a large enough part of the Parliamentary Conservative Party that her rigorous defence of Britain's national interests was proving counter-productive, though Michael Heseltine's failure to achieve the succession suggested that neither in Parliament nor in the party in the country was there any whole-hearted acceptance of a Euro-federalist position.[15]

What remains unclear for this period as for the preceding one is how far British politicians understood what their continental counterparts were seeking, how far they thought they were attaining their own ends and what British interests they believed were being preserved or could be preserved in a Europe on the Delors model. While such ignorance might have been excusable in the early stages of the Community when a whole new and unfamiliar set of ideas and institutions made difficult and unwelcome demands on politicians and civil servants with, as they saw it, more important and urgent demands on their time and energies, by the 1980s such excuses are harder to accept. Either one had to accept the ultimate defeatism of Edward Heath and his friends, and say that in the contemporary world an independent Britain made no sense, and that if one's destiny was to be just one of the provinces of a federal system one should organise one's affairs so as to make the best of it, or one had to argue that Britain's material and human resources were such that if free to make her own policies through her own parliamentary processes there was no need for such a sacrifice.[16]

For most of the time such clarity was not forthcoming. To denounce the whole process upon which Britain had entered was in most enlightened circles highly unfashionable.[17] It was to separate oneself from the political, administrative, academic and, above all, business elite. The last is the most important since just as during the referendum the money-bags were on the side of Europe, the short-term benefits of going along remained sufficient for many industrialists and financiers. The injury to the nation's morale and so ultimately to its economic prospects arising from the surrender of sovereignty was beyond their horizons. On the other hand the partisans of whole-hearted Europhilia were too well-aware of the basic hostility in the country towards such defeatism to proclaim their federalism in too open a fashion.

It was important for the British government to know not only where the continental Euro-federalists were agreed but also where they disagreed. If one reduces the thrust of the movement towards European 'integration' to the two principal countries, France and Germany – as one must, since none of the others would ever take a stand against them – it is clear that from the very beginning their interests and outlook were bound to be different and that they changed over time. For Germany after the war, the Community, like NATO and the WEU, was a route out of isolation and back into the comity of civilised nations. At that time France saw the Community as primarily a method of preventing a resurgent Germany from threatening its vital interests. But even when a relative balance was achieved there remained major dissimilarities. The de Gaulle–Adenauer agreement of January 1963 was not followed up, and the two countries' paths diverged. France, with its permanent seat on the UN Council and above all its '*force de frappe*', was both a European and a would-be world power. Germany, which had renounced all weapons of mass destruction and had a public opinion strongly allergic to power politics, was in quite a different situation. It had been put on its feet by the Americans, was open to American influence, looking to America to protect it against the Soviet power in the east and ultimately to assist in the 'reunification' which remained its long-term aspiration, though when Kohl became Chancellor still one which seemed a long way off.

In matters more directly affecting the internal affairs of the Community itself there were also differences. Fundamentally the French remained wedded to planning, protectionism and the purposeful intervention of the state in economic life. The Germans were closer to the Anglo-Saxons in seeing the virtues of free trade and a market-driven economy, though the philosophy of the 'Social Market' enabled them to allow considerable state activity in the social sphere. Finally, while German experience produced a fear of inflation as the overriding element in economic policy, French experience put a greater emphasis on keeping down the level of unemployment.

For these and other reasons, the policy of British governments had always to be to see which of the two countries was most likely to be open to persuasion about its particular needs. On the side of foreign policy and defence it was usually easier to see common ground with the French though this was not the case during the de Gaulle regime because of the French dislike of Britain's close relations with the United States in nuclear matters. In questions of economic policy the British had on the face of it more in common with the Germans – for long the only other net contributors to the Community budget and at least in theory more committed to free trade. On the other hand, the Common Agricultural Policy, the main source of the budget imbalance, was, while less important to the Germans than to the French, something to which for internal party-political reasons they felt they had to cling, for all its invidious impact upon living standards in Europe and the distortion it introduced into world trade. There was therefore always the question for British statesmen of whether they could persuade the French to take their side in some internal argument or whether they would do better to try to reach an understanding with the Germans. Bilateral meetings between the heads of the three governments remained important in the 1980s as in the 1970s. But any expectations placed upon such diplomacy had little prospect of success so long as both the Germans and the French believed that their basic objectives could be secured within the kind of Europe that Monnet had imagined and that Delors was trying to create.

Psychologically Kohl and Mitterrand, like Schmidt and Giscard d'Estaing, had made a leap which was impossible for Mrs Thatcher, if not for all her collaborators. When she referred to Britain's payments into the Community as 'our money' and therefore maintained that in some way Britain was entitled to get it back she was still speaking the language of independence. For the federalists this was nonsense; the whole point of the Community having its 'own' resources was to enable it to dispose of them for the common good.

Since Britain could not in the 1980s persuade the continental countries to go back on what they had in one form or another been practising for over thirty years, Britain was fighting a losing battle. Both the Single European Act and the Treaty of Maastricht were major British diplomatic defeats, although a good deal was done to counter that impression where the British public was concerned. By 1995, Lady Thatcher had admitted that it had been a mistake to go along with the Single European Act and professed to having been deceived into accepting it.[18] In 1995, John Major was still claiming that Maastricht had been a success on which British policy for Europe could still be based.

The major concentration of the British government in European matters in the early years of the Thatcher administration was on the Community budget. A solution at least for a time was reached at the Fontainebleau summit in June 1994.[19] What was neglected was the revival among the other members of the Community of the movement towards further integration. The Luxembourg Compromise defining the ultimate right of veto, adopted in 1966 to keep France under de Gaulle within the Community's machinery, was no longer of such interest to a France which under Mitterrand saw itself as a leader rather than a laggard in the Community's development. The intention to proceed in the federal direction was manifest in the Declaration on European Union reached at the Stuttgart summit in June 1983. 'This text', points out the then foreign secretary, 'was not legally binding but "only" declaratory; we attached less importance than most of our colleagues – less than we should have done – to this blueprint for the future.'[20]

Lady Thatcher explains Britain's adhesion in her memoirs by saying: 'I took the view that I could not quarrel with everything, and the documents had no legal force.' She assured the House of Commons that she did not in any way 'believe in a federated Europe' nor did 'that document'. It was clearly only subsequently that she realised that the

'high-flown language' of the declaration, as with later enun-
ciations of grand objectives, was 'the linguistic skeleton on
which so much institutional flesh would grow'.[21] While it is
true that no indication of what the 'wider objectives' of the
Community would be, the indication of the way opinion was
moving should no doubt have been taken more seriously.
Such at least is the view of Lord Cockfield.[22]

In fact the main area of interest had come to be the
completion of the 'single market' envisaged by the original
makers of the Community, coupled with the belief that if it
were to be brought about, further powers of decision-making and enforcement would need to be given to the central
institutions. The first attempt at moving ahead was the
'European Draft Treaty' approved by the European Parliament in 1984 but not pressed by the Italian presidency in
1985 when it suggested instead an intergovernmental conference to consider amendments to the treaties. It was clear
that what many of those concerned had in mind was not
only the single market but an extension of the Community's
role into other fields including monetary policy.[23]

At its crudest the difficulty faced by British politicians over
the next couple of years was that while Britain believed itself
to have much to gain by completing a single market, it was
only willing to make institutional changes, particularly the
extension of majority voting for this particular area of the
Community's activity; it did not wish to give it any new
powers in other fields. Such was certainly the view of
Margaret Thatcher. In these circumstances the role of Lord
Cockfield is on the face of it extraordinary, since his own
actions as well as the positions he took later on reveal him
to have been as dedicated a federalist as any continental
European and quite happy to work alongside Jacques Delors.

Why then did the Prime Minister, having found no
suitable role for him in her reshuffled cabinet after the
election of 1983, see fit to offer Cockfield a place as one of
the two British commissioners?

Lady Thatcher had thought he would be 'effective in
Brussels' and 'always paid tribute to the contribution he

made to the Single Market programme'. But in her view, 'unfortunately he tended to disregard the larger questions of politics – constitutional sovereignty, national sovereignty and the promptings of liberty'.[24] Lord Cockfield's account of his time at the Commission do not bear out this judgement. On the contrary, for him 'the larger questions' of politics were clearly of overriding importance; only the answers he gave were not those of the Prime Minister, nor, as far as one can know it, of the majority of his fellow-countrymen. He believed in full economic union as the only satisfactory future for the United Kingdom though he was prepared to wait rather longer than Delors and Chancellor Kohl for the political union which they thought immediately necessary.

What he does not seem to have done is to repudiate the goal itself; nor does he seem to have accepted the view that what was happening was precisely the slide into complete federalism which has been analysed in an earlier chapter. Indeed he repeated in his own book published as recently as 1994 the familiar fallacy that 'federalism' means something different in Europe to its ordinary usage. The confusion is shown by his statement: 'Germany is a Federal Republic and the concept of "federation" is regarded as the cornerstone and guarantee of democracy'; so of course it is for the Germans, and indeed for the Americans as he also claims.[25] What he does not bring himself to say, and this has been true of so many of the Europhiles, is that he is in favour of Britain becoming in relation to the Community institutions what Bavaria or Schleswig-Holstein are to the German federal government or North Dakota to the government at Washington. He claims in his book that the British media and British politicians concealed the truth about 'Europe' from the British public. The reverse is true; what were concealed were the consequences of the drive towards a European union which Lord Cockfield and his friends did their best to play down; so that even his own Prime Minister clearly had no real knowledge of his views.

The negotiations which culminated in the Single European Act were carried on under Delors's guiding hand and with much assistance from Cockfield. The entry into the

Community, effective in 1986, of Spain, Portugal and
Greece seemed an added reason for diminishing the power
of individual states to hold up the process of integration.
The proposals to go into such a treaty were drafted by
Cockfield in a White Paper just before the Milan summit of
June 1985. At that summit, Britain submitted proposals for
some form of cooperation in foreign policy which would not
detract from the ultimate right of states to go their own way.
It also suggested ways by which within the existing treaty
structure, additional efficiency might be brought into the
workings of the Community. But the Prime Minister found
that the pressure for an intergovernmental conference was
too strong to be resisted.[26]

In the interim between the Milan Council and the Luxembourg Council in December, further proposals were put
on the agenda. Delors wished to include economic and
monetary union but was opposed by the Germans as well as
the British. The Luxembourg summit was however again
the occasion of a Franco-German bargain brokered by
Delors. Germany accepted a mention of the 1972 European
Community's commitment to economic and monetary
union and France agreed to the freedom of capital movements.[27] The course of discussions produced two documents,
one covering amendments to the Treaty of Rome, the Single
European Act, the other an intergovernmental agreement
setting up arrangements for cooperation on foreign policy.

The British government was successful in limiting some
applications of the new agreements arising from its island
status and resisted Cockfield's ideas on the harmonising of
taxes. It thus felt free to commend the Single European Act
to Parliament where the ratification went through without
difficulty in April 1986. Thereafter some disillusion set in
although the actual timetable for the single market measures
did go according to plan.

What the British government discovered, according to
Geoffrey Howe, was that they were facing 'on some social
and environmental matters a more extensive use of Community powers' than they had regarded as foreseeable or
legitimate. It was due, in his view, 'largely to the way in

which the habit of sharing sovereignty within the Community extended itself in the mere process of working together'. What he does not refer to is the fact that the Single European Act, like the Treaty of Rome itself, would provide new material for a Court ever on the lookout for occasions to assert the supremacy of Community law.

What Lord Howe does admit is that the Single European Act, contrary to what both he and the Prime Minister believed did affect the Luxembourg Compromise, not in so many words – since the compromise itself had no legal status – but by emphasising the practice of majority voting which subsequently took place to an ever increasing extent.[28] As already noted, the Single European Act was in retrospect something that on the whole Margaret Thatcher came to regret:

> The first fruits of what would be called the Single European Act were good for Britain. At last, I felt, we were going to get the Community back on course, concentrating on its role as a huge market, with all the opportunities that would bring to our industries. Advantages will indeed flow from that achievement well into the future even though harmonization and standardization regularly threaten to become ends in themselves. The trouble was – and I must give full credit to those Tories who warned of this at the time – that the new powers the Commission received only seemed to whet its appetite.[29]

It is of course true that the Commission itself under Delors was an important engine of centralisation and that its spirit seemed to embrace new commissioners whatever their political provenance. When Mrs Thatcher did not nominate Cockfield for a second term – quite understandably – his replacement, another ex-cabinet minister, Sir Leon Brittan, soon revealed himself a no less ardent defender of the Community and its prerogatives. When Delors himself retired, John Major, who had by then succeeded Mrs Thatcher as Prime Minister, cast a British veto against the Franco-German agreement that his successor should be the Belgian Prime Minister Jean-Luc Dehaene on the ground that he was too federalist. The individual to whose nomination he did agree, Jacques Santer, the Prime Minister of Luxembourg, turned out to be no less imbued with the federal faith.[30]

Neither the Commission nor the Court could have pushed for further steps towards a completely federal structure had this not been the desire of important member states. This, as Lady Thatcher herself shows in her account of the London summit of December 1986, was visible even before the Single European Act came into effect on 1 July 1987. There had been in 1985–6 'a profound shift in the kind of Europe that was taking shape . . . a Franco-German bloc with its own agenda had re-emerged to set the direction of the Community'.[31]

The Single European Act did not put an end to the activity of Delors and his allies. In 1988, the idea of economic and monetary union was again revived and was looked at in depth by a committee headed by Delors himself. With the conversion of the Germans to the idea, it was clearly once more on the agenda. By 1989 attention was also being paid to less well-defined projects to remedy what were seen as weaknesses in the existing Community arrangements. One was to tackle the 'democratic deficit' by giving greater powers to the European Parliament – favoured by the Germans, Italians, Belgians and Dutch though less attractive to the French. The upheavals in eastern and central Europe focused attention on what were held to be the inadequacies of the current machinery for political cooperation. Austria's application for membership gave point to the whole question of a further expansion of the Community and the new institutional arrangements which might be held to follow from it. Germany, which had been wary of closer political union, became more favourable once reunification had removed the fear that the Community might stand in the way of national aspirations.[32]

It was realised not least by Delors himself that much if not all of this programme would not be acceptable to the British, but it would be wrong to see 'Europe' as at the heart of British politics in these years. For this fact a number of reasons could be suggested. First, Britain's conception of its own foreign policy priorities made for more attention to what was actually happening in the wider world than to plans for 'Europe'. A few dates need to be kept in mind. On 12 March 1985, Gorbachev became leader of the Soviet Communist Party and so *de facto* ruler of the Soviet Union. On 19–21 November that year he had his first summit with Reagan. On 11–12 October, 1986 Gorbachev and Reagan met at Reykjavik, raising some fears among the United States' allies that the liquidation of the 'cold war' was progressing faster than was safe. On 7–8 December 1987 a further Gorbachev–Reagan summit included the signature of a treaty on the elimination of their intermediate and short-range missiles in Europe. On 29 May – 1 June 1988 the two leaders met in Moscow and they met again at the United Nations in December. While these changes in the relations between the Soviet Union and the United States were taking place, Gorbachev was also placing his relations with the two Germanies on a new footing and indicating a loosening of the political ties that constrained the Soviet allies in the Warsaw Pact.

Quite apart from the demands that these events made upon the time and attention of British ministers, there were internal explanations as to why so little attention was paid to the transformation being sought in the affairs of the Community. It could almost be said that the British constitutional system was itself not working according to its own principles. The 'Westminster model' depends upon a dialogue between government and opposition during which both appeal to the country for its verdict on their contrasting policies. But in the years under review, the opposition was unable to make much of such opportunities. Under Foot and the early Kinnock it was clearly unelectable and its commitment to an anti-integrationist position not of great relevance.

The other principal of assumption was that the Prime Minister's principal colleagues were of one mind and that the policies they followed would in their turn appeal to the rank and file. On the latter point one need only point to the mismanagement of the 'community charge' or 'poll tax' which as it was implemented began to look like a vote-loser and was as important in bringing about the downfall of Margaret Thatcher as the differences over 'Europe'. But it was on the latter that the cabinet solidarity foundered.

The two key figures were Geoffrey Howe, foreign secretary since 1983, and Nigel Lawson who then succeeded him as chancellor of the exchequer. Yet their positions on the Community were far from identical. Lawson believed that the Single European Act could benefit Britain by making it possible to transform the customs union into a truly single market. On the other hand, he did not favour monetary union which he held to be incompatible with national sovereignty, nor did he go along with Cockfield in holding that tax harmonisation was a prerequisite for the functioning of the single market. His vision of an outward-looking Europe was very far removed from the Delors emphasis on further integration between the existing Twelve. Where he differed from Mrs Thatcher was in his belief that his objective of low inflation could best be served by Britain's entry into the ERM, putting a stable exchange rate at the centre of the Treasury's concern.[33]

It was on the question of joining the ERM that Lawson found himself aligned with Howe and equally put out when Mrs Thatcher rejected their recommendation in the autumn of 1985. Yet although there were, as we have seen, reservations in Howe's enthusiasm for Euro-federalism he, unlike Lawson, regarded the ERM as a step on the road to EMU – a single currency – to which Lawson was opposed, seeing ERM rather as an alternative. What both agreed upon was the need to take a more conciliatory tone towards the Commission and its initiatives and the other heads of government. They both deplored Mrs Thatcher's insistence that it was only by standing up to pressure even when Britain stood alone that its objectives could be met.

It was a combination of these factors that produced their joint threat of resignation before the Madrid summit in June 1989 which led Mrs Thatcher in fact to agree that subject to some conditions the UK would join the ERM as it did in

October 1990, and also to an inter-governmental conference on EMU. But this success for the two ministers was not something which chimed in with Mrs Thatcher's view of the world, and it was followed by the demotion of Geoffrey Howe from the FCO to the leadership of the House. In October, Lawson himself resigned.

It is clear that Mrs Thatcher's view of Europe and its future remained haunted by the fear of German domination. It is also clear that she had an alternative vision to that of Delors, Mitterrand and Kohl. Delors's position was set out in his speech to the TUC in September 1988. Lawson informs us that the idea of his coming came from the FCO which thought it would help to decrease Labour hostility to Britain's involvement with the Community.[34] What it did was to assist the process already in train by which the Labour Party was moving towards its later pro-European stance. The idea of a 'social Europe' was not new – the Messina communiqué of June 1955 had talked of the 'progressive harmonization of social policies' among the future members of the proposed European Community.[35] But its injection now was to be of importance in all that followed. The Labour Party began to appreciate that the new form of Euro-federalism with its emphasis on social policy and workers' rights could be a better instrument with which to oppose a Conservative government than the earlier demands to end the relationship. The later Kinnock, John Smith and Tony Blair were to follow this path with increasing enthusiasm.

Mrs Thatcher's speech at Bruges on 20 September 1988 gave a picture of a Europe of freely cooperating nation states dedicated to deregulation, market economics and seeing its ultimate defence as still lying with NATO. Such a Europe gave little scope for the grandiose plans of the Delors Commission: 'We have not successfully rolled back the frontiers of the State in Britain only to see them reimposed at the Community level.'

Lawson suggests that the actual content of the speech was widely acceptable but that the coverage instigated by the Prime Minister's press secretary emphasised the negative aspects and a tone of hostility to the Community.[36] The Euro-elections of June 1989 were also fought in a negative fashion with the attack on a 'diet of Brussels'. Labour did not in fact fight the election on European issues but on domestic issues; however the gains it achieved made its contingent of MEPs the largest in the socialist group which in turn contributed to the party's swing towards a pro-European position.[37]

How far one can go along with the view that Delors's own aim in the hectic proclamation of new integrationist policies in 1989 was to bring about the fall of Mrs Thatcher must depend upon further evidence being forthcoming.[38] It is clearly the case that her conduct at and after the extra Rome meeting of the European Council in October 1990 was the proximate cause of Howe's resignation on 1 November.[39] Although no formal decisions were taken at Rome nor could be, it was clear that the Christian Democrat–Socialist coalition which Delors had mustered was going for a single currency and political integration whatever Britain's objections, and that the alternative idea on the monetary side, the 'hard ecu' proposed by Lawson's successor as Chancellor, John Major, was not going to be looked at. Mrs Thatcher saw that the ultimate battle for the future of the Community had now been joined. When she came to report on Rome to the House of Commons she made it clear that Britain would not accept the imposition of a single currency – 'this government believes in the pound sterling'. Nor would she countenance Delors's project for remodelling the Community's institutions in an unmistakably federal direction, by turning the Parliament into the Community's House of Representatives, the Council of Ministers into a Senate and the Commission into its Executive. 'No, no, no', she declared.[40]

Howe's resignation speech confirmed that his differences with the Prime Minister were of substance, not just style.[41] He criticised her negative attitude to all that came from Europe and her unwillingness even to give full endorsement to the 'hard ecu' proposals. The speech was for the most part in the familiar Europhile vein. Macmillan had been right to see Britain's future as lying in an active participation in the building of a new Europe to which Britain could make a constructive contribution. The refusal to contemplate membership of an economic and monetary union was the final example of the negative attitude which the Prime Minister had espoused against much cabinet advice.

It cannot be estimated with accuracy how far the challenge to Mrs Thatcher's leadership that followed from Michael Heseltine was triggered by similar considerations. Still less can one assert with confidence that members of Parliament who supported him on the first ballot were moved by pro-European sentiment rather than by their fears for their own seats in the light of domestic problems – the poll tax in particular – and the desire for a new leadership to improve their chances whenever the next election came.

How far the European issue was involved in the proceedings which led to Mrs Thatcher's failure to secure the necessary quota of votes to get through on the first ballot and her decision on the advice of most of her colleagues not to fight the second ballot is again something impossible to reckon with certainty. The events were part of parliamentary and party history and only indirectly part of Britain's relations with Europe. What is striking is that even in so far as there was a European aspect to the matter – as Howe saw it – there was even now more concentration on some secondary issues at the expense of the central one, the march of federalism.

It was not the recasting of institutions upon which Delors and his allies relied but his projects for expanding the area of the Community's competence and hence of Community expenditure.[42] If there was machinery for transferring funds from tax payers in one country to other countries, the essence of a federal structure was already in being. Spaniards, Portuguese, Irishmen and Greeks might feel as passionately committed to their own national identity as Mrs Thatcher was to Britain's; but as net recipients of the Community's largesse they would not rock the boat. On the other hand, even Mrs Thatcher and her closest associates were not ready to suggest that the whole venture had been a mistake or to question what had been given away in Britain's entry terms – her historic fishing grounds for instance, handed over to the Community by Heath as a kind of dowry.

We do know that once Mrs Thatcher had decided to step down she was determined to block the accession of Michael Heseltine whom she regarded as too committed to the European cause and put her influence behind John Major as the most likely alternative candidate whom she would find acceptable. Five years later it is still difficult to know the extent of John Major's commitment to a particular line on Europe or how far his original stance has been affected by the vast changes that have taken place in the interim, some of Britain's making, some not. Since he kept Douglas Hurd as foreign secretary the continuity of British diplomacy, in substance if not in style, seemed to be assured. Whether Major's short tenure of the Foreign Office between Howe's departure and Hurd's taking over gave him any inkling of the degree to which the Office itself was committed to a Community position it is too early to say.

What the Major–Hurd team did do was to accept the way the Community appeared to be going and to see how far Britain's individual national requirements could be met. It was a question of mending fences with countries and individuals. Where Germany was concerned, it was possible to build upon the work the Conservative Party chairman, Kenneth Baker, had done in Mrs Thatcher's final year in building links with the CDU.[43] In May 1990 he attended the CDU rally at which the party East and West found itself united. The way was thus paved for Major as Prime Minister to make in March 1991 his famous address to the Konrad Adenauer Foundation which included the much-quoted remark that 'I want us to be where we belong at the very heart of Europe, working with our partners in building the future'. Kenneth Baker summed up the difference between the two Prime Ministers as John wanting to be at the heart of Europe while Margaret appeared to prefer being at its throat.[44]

What was important was not the rhetoric but the pursuit of national goals, there being every indication that Conservative worries about the direction of the Community and in particular about the proposed single currency were as acute as ever. On the whole the Major–Hurd team could claim some achievements. First Kohl and then Mitterrand gave undertakings that no decisions would be reached at the European Council scheduled for Luxembourg in June. By the time the issues came to be tied up at the Maastricht Conference in December, the lines of a compromise had been worked out. Major's balance between the Euro-enthusiasts and the Euro-sceptics was by now a feature of any possible Conservative cabinet as well as of the party in Parliament and in the country.

The Maastricht Treaty made a number of important additions to the Treaty of Rome by which the original Communities were absorbed into a new structure, the European Union.[45] Its functioning was set to be monitored and any needful changes made at an intergovernmental conference due to begin in the spring of 1997. To the formal economic objectives of the original communities, there were to be added machinery for arriving at a common foreign policy, looking ultimately to a common defence, a formalization of the habit of foreign policy consultations that had grown up between member states. In addition a number of functions exercised by ministers of home affairs or ministers of justice in the member states were to be brought within its purview. British objections to a further acquisition of power by the existing community institutions − Commission, Court and Parliament − were met by providing that the Union should have a three-pillared structure. The first pillar − the existing institutions − would handle economic and social issues. The second and third pillars, which would be intergovernmental, would handle law and order issues and, separately foreign affairs and defence. The last was likely to be the most controversial area since continental enthusiasts for integration wished the Union to take over the western Europe's long-standing machinery for handling defence matter, while Britain wished the links between WEU and Nato to remain in place.

While the commitment to freedom of movement was part of the Community concept, Britain had not taken part in the Schengen Convention of 1990 by which a number of adjacent continental countries undertook to dismantle all border controls. On the other hand, Britain did not stay aloof from the commitment to create a common European citizenship which had a symbolic importance, as well as the practical consequence of conferring the franchise in local government and European elections to citizens of other member states in the country in which they happened to reside. The fact that the Queen would become a 'citizen of Europe' as well as her subjects was the foundation of the charge of treason brought in English and Scottish courts against the ministers who had signed the treaty, and provided yet another angle from which to challenge the validity of the successive sacrifices of British sovereignty from the original accession to the Treaty of Rome. While these cases were clearly not going to succeed, the sovereignty of Parliament issue could yet arise should a British government seek to leave the Union whose basic instruments make no provision for their denunciation any more than secession is allowed for by the Constitution of the United States.[46]

One is bound to ask whether the Prime Minister and his colleagues fully understood that it made little sense to talk about resisting federalism while accepting the notion of common citizenship or whether they reckoned that it would be hard to resist calls for the dismantling of all entry controls from the continent if other European citizens were to claim that their right of free entry was being impeded. Or did they know what they were doing but kept the knowledge to themselves?

What was done was to direct parliamentary and public attention to the two points where Britain had succeeded in getting special treatment, enabling Major to claim 'game, set and match'. One was to enable Britain to defer a decision on entering EMU until the third stage, which was to see the installation of a single currency, had arrived. Britain was still to take part in the two earlier stages of the process although it was clear that the 'opt-out' made it difficult for Britain to

claim London as the headquarters of the new pan-European
monetary institutions. The other was to stay outside the
commitment to the 'social chapter'.

The social chapter of the treaty embodied the 'social
charter' agreed upon in 1989 when social policy was already
an important part of the Community's activity. Britain had
agreed to allow the provisions for majority voting in the
Single European Act to apply to common policies concern-
ing health and safety at work. Since resistance to the
imposition upon British industry and commerce of the
prevalent continental arrangements for employer–employee
relationships and other facets of Christian Democrat–Socialist interventionism, Major could not go further along this
line without risking the defeat of the whole treaty when
it came before Parliament. Despite the unhappiness of
Germany and France, the 'social protocol' was added to
the treaty enabling the other eleven countries to adopt
the provisions of the social charter without British participation.

The willingness of other countries and the Commission to
accept the protocol was no doubt largely due to the knowledge that given the vague language of the Treaty of Rome,
and the benign attitude of the Luxembourg Court towards
Community legislation under the 'harmonisation' umbrella,
ways would be found of preventing this 'opt-out' from being
used to put British firms in a more competitive position and
the British economy from attracting a high proportion of the
inward investment coming into the Community.

From the more narrowly political point of view, the social
protocol provided the final excuse the Labour Party needed
to justify its new pro-European position. Delors's speech to
the TUC had amply paid off. There was henceforth hardly
to be a debate on 'Europe' in which the Labour protagonists
did not make much of the denial of 'rights' to the British
working men and women which their continental counterparts enjoyed to the full.

In the light of these 'triumphs' the British were prepared
to accept the creation of the 'cohesion' fund by which the
poorer countries were to be assisted financially to enable

them to fulfil the criteria set out in the treaty for adhesion to EMU, and the setting up of a Committee of the Regions which would give another sounding-board to the government's critics on the peripheries of the United Kingdom.

The relation of the treaty's provision that 'subsidiarity' should be the guiding principle of the Union's future activity to the general endorsement of a federal model has been dealt with in an earlier chapter. Although it was partially intended to protect an existing federal system, that of Germany, by reassuring the German Länder, it was never capable of bearing the weight that government spokesmen defending the treaty in Britain were to place upon it. It was not a principle intended to act as a dike against further Community legislation creeping into, as it was said, 'the nooks and crannies' of national life.

When the history of the Major administration comes to be written with full access to the sources, one question that will be asked is how Michael Heseltine, President of the Board of Trade and subsequently Deputy Prime Minister, a noted and powerful advocate of 'deregulation', should at the same time have remained on the Europhile wing of the cabinet, since Brussels was adding to the quota of regulations as fast or faster than Heseltine could get rid of them. One could think of him as a reverse Penelope, restoring at night what he had unravelled during the day.[47]

It would however be right to record that when the treaty was signed on 7 February 1992, it did appear that the view that Britain had attained its objectives was the predominant one and that not a great deal of serious opposition was to be expected. Although the European theme was not prominent in the general election held in April 1992 which was won by the Conservatives on the issue, it would seem, of Labour's financial credibility, it may be that for some voters Major's performance at Maastricht did appear to herald a period in which Britain would play a leading role in Europe's reaction to an increasingly doubtful economic and political outlook. More important was the reduction in the Conservatives' overall majority which meant that party unity would be more crucial than ever.

For the moment, the omens for Maastricht appeared good. On May 12, the Queen gave her first address to the European Parliament to whose powers Maastricht had made some significant additions. She was the last head of a member state of the Community to go to Strasbourg, and the first to do so as a presumptive 'European citizen', though this aspect of the matter was hardly stressed.

On 21 May the House of Commons approved the Maastricht Treaty Bill by 336 votes to 92. The low total is explained by the fact that the Labour Party indicated its anger at the opt-out from the social chapter by abstaining. Twenty-two Conservatives and 59 Labour MPs voted against. It seemed more of a gesture than a political act. Maastricht for the Europhile enthusiast for European Union looked like the end of the beginning; within quite a short space of time, it was looking like the beginning of the end.

6 Britain, France and European Union

British reluctance to merge its national identity in an integrated Europe, whether styled a European Union or a United States of Europe, was an obvious consequence of a historical experience very different from that of its continental neighbours and of institutions, political and legal, that were also unique. Its attitudes were also shaped by its more recent experience in the Second World War, the conclusions drawn from the way in which survival and ultimately victory had been achieved, and the massive domestic and external tasks that faced it. But it would be equally mistaken to see the continental countries that made up the original Six and the later Fifteen as having so much in common that their rulers did not need to have regard to their national interests, as perceived by their electorates, when calculating their own attitudes to the process of constructing the new Europe.

Half a century has not reduced these differences. Even after the Treaty of Maastricht laid it down that the citizens of all its signatories and of those states admitted into the European Union in future would be 'citizens of Europe', that was not how any but a few eccentric ideologues actually saw themselves. Individuals continued to see themselves as British, French, German, Italian, Spanish, Dutch and so forth. There are still no 'Europeans', a fact which the European Parliament itself amply illustrates in its actual handling of affairs. Should the Scottish Nationalists get their way and Scotland become a separate member of the European Union, Scottish ministers and officials will surely show a like concern in the furthering of Scottish objectives.

From the point of view of the British record it is not necessary to deal with each individual country in detail.[1] Despite Britain's historic interest in the Low Countries and its involvement in different ways with the countries of the Mediterranean, what has been dominant in British thinking

113

has been the roles of France and Germany within the new
European system and of the United States and the reformed
Soviet Union (Russia) outside it. Above all, the history of
these fifty years can be seen in terms of an Anglo-French
dialogue. In 1995 Anglo-French relations remain at the
heart of British foreign and military policy as they were in
1945 when it was only five years since the attempt to keep
France in the war by means of an Anglo-French union had
been frustrated by French defeatism in the face of the
seemingly irresistible German advance.[2]

The common perception has been that France has been
committed to the integrationist drive and that this commitment has general support. Such beliefs were dented by the
narrowness of the margin by which the French electorate
agreed in a referendum to the ratification of the Treaty of
Maastricht – a quarter of a million votes the other way
would have produced a negative. And the course of the
French presidential election in 1995 indicated that the
doubts had not been stilled. The two leading French statesmen most closely associated with a 'pro-European' position,
Giscard d'Estaing and Raymond Barre, did not put their
names forward. None of the three leading candidates based
their campaigns upon this issue and there was strong
support for candidates on both the extreme wings of French
politics who were overtly hostile to further integration –
though their votes were admittedly secured for other reasons
as well.

The other perception of the French position owes much
no doubt to the prominence in the history of the European
Communities of two Frenchmen, Jean Monnet and Jacques
Delors.[3] Of course there had been ever since French political life was reanimated after the liberation an important
knot of people who believed that the nation could and
should be transcended and for whom therefore the construction of 'Europe' was a primary goal. This was true both
when France was in the lead in the 1945–57 period and
again during the period of Mitterrand's presidency when
France gave strong support to Delors's reactivation of the
Community's institutions. It was clear even to the most

pro-European members of Mitterrand's entourage that the French would still need to be persuaded that European integration could be reconciled with their own material interests.[4]

France's position throughout the fifty years was affected both in respect of elite opinion and among the public at large by assumptions that went back as in Britain's case deep into the country's history. Unlike Germany and Italy where their modern statehood was the outcome of national movements, the French nation was itself the product of the action of the state itself over something like a millenium. The various portions of what went to make up the 'hexagon' had been assembled largely through the use of military force by the kings of France, and were further extended and consolidated by the Republican and Napoleonic regimes that succeeded them.

The centralisation of authority, incomplete at the time of the Revolution, was further developed under the subsequent regimes and, under the Third Republic, the process of 'creating Frenchmen' was completed by the introduction of compulsory military service and of a universal largely state-provided education in the standard language. While the British sense of identity was the product of geography and history, and German identity of a sense of racial, linguistic and cultural affinities, French identity was willed by France's rulers. Most definitions of the 'nation state' come down to descriptions of France.

The process has never been completed. Bretons and Alsaciens remain outside the linguistic consensus and the territory of the Languedoc has preserved its distance from the dominant France of the north and east. Indeed some protagonists of European integration hope to build upon this difference. Elizabeth Guigou suggests from her Provençal angle that the regions of south-eastern and south-western France should come together with their neighbours over the Italian and Spanish frontiers and with North Africa to create a focus of economic and cultural activity embracing the whole western Mediterranean to counterbalance those parts of France more closely linked to the Rhenish axis of the

Community. It might be pointed out in passing that in the brief time since Madame Guigou published her reflections, political developments as indicated in both national and local elections suggest that opposition to the degree of inward migration from North Africa far outweighs any thought of the benefits that might be obtained from such a development. While France has been more hospitable than some European countries to immigrants and readier to undertake the task of turning them also into 'Frenchmen' within a generation or two, that tolerance has now come under severe strain. Catholic Poles are one thing – Moslem Algerians another.

Aside from regional differences, different sections of French society interpreted their sense of nationality in different ways. The first of these was the consequence of the impact upon France of the Reformation and Counter-Reformation. The historian of the Third Republic, Sir Denis Brogan, was wont to say that he knew of at least one French constituency where voting behaviour was determined by whether one was for or against the revocation of the Edict of Nantes. That event made France an adherent of the Catholic side in the great divide which had dominated the politics of western and central Europe since the time of Luther and Calvin. The Enlightenment and the Revolution introduced a further division between the idea of a secular state and those who cherished France's role as the favoured daughter of the Church.

The French Revolution also linked the new idea of a wholly secular state with the subordination of the provinces to central government. It is not without interest that the strongly anti-European candidate of the right in the presidential election of 1995 – Philippe de Villiers – should have polled so strongly in the Vendée, the last seat of resistance to Jacobin Paris.

The French Revolution and its sequels in 1848 and 1870 also brought about a new division between socialist and non-socialist approaches to the problems of industrial society. The Russian Revolution – a cardinal event in French history – divided the socialist camp itself into discordant factions as was still all too evident at the time of the liberation.

The Third Republic lasted longer than any other regime since the overthrow of monarchical absolutism; it also saw the expansion and consolidation of France's overseas empire which was to play so important a part in the thinking of France's leaders after 1945. But it was an era of considerable instability and of successive crises of which the most notorious, the Dreyfus affair, was to echo until the end of the Republic and after. The Vichy regime was indeed the product of external defeat but its installation was at the same time a deliberate choice, since resistance based on the overseas empire did present an alternative course of action. It was also a choice which reversed what had been the general tenor of politics under the Third Republic by opting for the reintegration of the Right and with it of the Catholic Church into the heart of the body politic.[5]

Since the move towards a European community linking France, Germany, Italy and the Low Countries was largely the work of Catholic statesmen, this experience helps to explain the strong revulsion of part of the Left against their handiwork. It was the Church which had brought about the triple alliance between Adenauer, Schuman and de Gasperi – 'trois tonsures sous la même calotte'.[6]

While the impetus to the creation of the new European institutions was in essence political, the means to integration were economic and much of the debate was from the beginning conducted in economic terms. Here another legacy from the French past has proved of enduring significance and that is the French commitment to a positive role for the state in economic matters – Colbertism as it is known for shorthand purposes – which involved both protectionism and the conscious planning of industry. It is here that the contrast with Britain is seen at its most acute. Given France's lavish endowment with natural resources, foreign trade never acquired the significance that it did in Britain. In a debate in the French National Assembly on 27 June 1851 Adolphe Tuiers, who was destined to be one of the founding fathers of the Third Republic, referred to Britain's recent repeal of the Corn Laws as imprudent and went on to declare 'free trade's underlying doctrine of laissez-faire to be a blasphemy against God's design for civilization which had given the temperate zone the intelligence whereby the raw products of the rest of the world could be brought to their perfection before being sent back to their places of origin'.[7]

The British free-traders would not have dissented from the general notion that it was the processing of materials acquired overseas that was essential to their country's prosperity; their view was that what was needed both in respect of raw materials and foodstuffs could be acquired as the result of the ordinary workings of the commercial markets, provided that naval power could be relied upon to safeguard the passage of merchant shipping, and when the alternative of an imperial system enforced by protectionist measures was presented, whether at the turn of the century or between the wars, it was rejected – the Ottawa agreements represented only a mild degree of preference for Empire and Commonwealth products. The French preferred a system in which the metropole and the overseas territories could be seen as part of a single system directed by the French government in the interests of the whole.

How imperial policy would have developed in the event of an Anglo-French union is a matter for speculation but the course of the war clearly enhanced the value of the French empire in the eyes of most Frenchmen, and while Britain's postwar Labour government set in train a process that was within less than a quarter of a century to see the dissolution of most of the imperial system, French governments, including those dominated by socialists, were to spend much of their energies and much of the national substance in trying to preserve their imperial authority first in the Middle East, then in Indo-China and finally, until de Gaulle's decision to liquidate the Algerian war, in North Africa.

From the point of view of France's participation in the moves towards European integration the imperial aspect cannot be overlooked.[8] The French military attached much importance to the incorporation of the French imperial periphery in any arrangements made for European defence which caused them to question some of the proposals for an integrated western army until their concerns shifted to the creation and maintenance of a French nuclear deterrent.[9]

On the economic side of the negotiations which led to the Treaty of Rome, France's strong bargaining position enabled her to secure from her partners preferential treatment for what remained of her colonial possessions in sub-Saharan Africa, the Caribbean and the Indian and Pacific Oceans. The expansion of the Communities did not lessen France's insistence on these points and while in the 1980s the Commonwealth was largely a shadow and British colonial possessions mere dots on the map, France maintained in fact if not in name a sizeable empire in sub-Saharan Africa still largely dependent upon the French economy and still relying for its security on French military strength. Relations with francophone Africa were among the attributes of French presidential power most closely guarded by President Mitterrand.

In the negotiations of the immediate postwar period these long-term differences between Britain and France which we can see more clearly in retrospect were of course overshadowed by the desperate need to find solutions to their economic and social problems with which they were confronted, to which their traditional modes of approach were not necessarily the most relevant and which depended for their solution, at least in the short term, upon the goodwill of the United States, impelled to offer assistance in part at least by the fears of the alternative communist solutions under Soviet patronage.[10]

Some differences can be seen in France between the attitudes of the reconstituted political elite and the higher echelons of the civil service. The latter were keen to find a way of bringing Britain – a leading player in the OEEC, the organisation for allocating Marshall Aid and negotiating the agreements on policy springing from it – into some wider and more permanent organisation for handling the economy of western Europe. In their minds this demanded some degree of planned specialisation which fitted in well with the

French bias towards planning.[11] The British, lacking confidence in what might happen and with recent experience of being cut off from Europe, were for the time being keen on self-sufficiency. A sizeable proportion of the French political elite had less expectation of what Britain could contribute and were open to the persuasion of Jean Monnet and others of his circle that the key to recovery was to be found in the coming together of the mining and steel capacity in the Ruhr, Lorraine, the Saar and Belgium – the Coal and Steel Community finally achieved in 1950.

It is clear that the French found negotiations even with their recent enemies more comfortable than those with the British with whom they were however at the same time engaged in building up defence cooperation culminating in both countries' membership of NATO. One reason for the difference was to remain valid in the 1940s – that was or has been seen as the French preference, shared with their continental neighbours, for agreements in broad general terms in contrast to the British preference for concrete statements about specific obligations and how they were to be met. It was admittedly the British unwillingness to accept a prior commitment to the proposal for the Coal and Steel Community prior to negotiating upon its details that excluded it from the original grouping of the Six. It has been consistently argued by the 'pro-European' elements in British public life that Britain should have clambered on the band-wagon at this stage and would by so doing have been in a position to influence the future activities of the European institutions in its own interests. As has been pointed out, experience after Britain's accession to the Communities does not suggest that British ideas can make their way where the original Six and in particular the French and the Germans have different goals in mind. But the historian must ask whether the offer of participation was made in good faith. Every indication is that this was not the case. The account by René Massigli, France's ambassador in London at the time and the principal channel of communication between the two governments, shows clearly that Monnet knew perfectly well that he was asking for a commitment which no British government could accept. He was quite content to leave Britain out in the confidence that sooner or later it would come along and fit into a system of which he would have been the architect.[12]

It must be remembered that the mixing up of French and German affairs as the way of ending their long history of conflict was by no means universally accepted among French political leaders. Many, particularly on the Left, still hoped that an arrangement with the Russians could keep Germany in subordination to French interests and this aspect of the matter came even more prominently to the fore when the Coal and Steel Community was followed by the project for a Defence Community.[13]

What became the Gaullist approach to the French situation was to try to assert France's place among the Great Powers. For this purpose the balancing of the Soviet Union against a purely American orientation seemed to make sense, although efforts in that direction were clearly hampered by the need simultaneously to reduce the strength of the Communist Party in France's internal affairs. But acceptance of France's claim to such a status depended upon the Americans who were determined to deny France's participation in some kind of three-power directorate within NATO. However often the spirit of Lafayette might be invoked the Americans remained convinced that France's days of greatness had ended in 1940 and could not return.

France therefore remained throughout what became the 'Cold War' dependent upon the United States for her ultimate defence while at the same time doubting whether that link could be relied upon in all circumstances.

The ambivalent stance towards the United States which outlived the de Gaulle era and was not determined by de Gaulle's experiences at Roosevelt's hands[14] was fortified by something particular to the French – their increasing cultural defensiveness centred upon the preservation of the privileged position that the French language had acquired in international discourse since the seventeenth century. English now represented a major threat to that position and sensitivity to Anglo-Saxon dominance in the cultural do-

main remained a constant of French attitudes and reached
new heights in the Mitterrand era when it was combined
with the more mundane protectionism of the French film
industry.

An Anglo-Saxon hegemony was not a concept which
attracted the Americans themselves. They were no more
inclined to give a special great-power status to the British
than to the French – both were seen as the bearers of an
old-fashioned imperialism to which the Americans were
hostile.

What the Americans wanted in the period from 1945 to
1948 was to remedy Europe's economic weakness and
consequent vulnerability to Soviet-sponsored communism
by bringing into use as soon as possible the economic
strength of Germany. When after 1948, the emphasis shifted
to the possibility of a direct military threat, the object was
to get German strength put back in the balance. The moves
towards a Coal and Steel Community and, after that was
achieved, towards a European Defence Community involving Germany made a direct appeal to the United States.
And the federal language in which the rhetoric of the
Monnet circle indulged chimed in with the United States'
belief that its own federal institutions should have a universal appeal.[15]

Nevertheless, however powerful and ruthless American
diplomacy was, it could only work with what was available.
The choice that France made and which produced after
many twists and turns the European Union of Maastricht
was a choice in foreign policy. The opportunity of a union
with Britain rejected in 1940 proved decisive. Vichy was not
simply a choice within the framework of French domestic
politics – revenge on the Dreyfusards – it was also a choice
in foreign policy. Since the alliance on which French policy
had been based had failed and Germany was now master of
the continent, it was necessary to make the best deal that
one could. For some at Vichy there was an element of
attentisme, no doubt, but for Pierre Laval and others, it was
seen as a rational and perhaps permanent commitment. If
France could no longer hope to be the dominant power in

Europe, perhaps it could at least fulfil the role of Germany's principal adjutant. The readiness of the Americans to over-look this aspect of the matter and its effect internally in France amply justifies de Gaulle's attitude towards them.

The choice as it presented itself in the post-war years was a different one. Could France now be the senior partner in a continental European bloc? Since Germany was going to be allowed to revive could this revival be reconciled with France's needs? It was the conviction of the French federa-lists of the Monnet school that this could be done if the new Germany was locked into supranational institutions where France, through her ties to the other members of such a set of institutions, could hold the upper hand.[16] In the begin-ning was the Coal and Steel Community. The credit for its creation has gone to Jean Monnet but, as René Massigli pointed out, there can be no doubt but that the origins of the Schuman Plan were American.[17]

Monnet's service was to persuade Robert Schuman, a man less confident of the wisdom of purely institutional solutions, to link up with his fellow Lotharingian Adenauer and with de Gasperi, a relic of Habsburg Europe, to put the necessary political drive behind the new concept.

The way in which to handle the French aspect of Britain's European problem is to realise that we are dealing with a number of different French approaches to 'Europe' which varied over the years as new groups and parties and factions formed and reformed. On the whole it is not difficult to distinguish among them the enduring element of Monnet's collaborators and supporters, a number of whom have left their own accounts of their contributions.[18] The Gaullist camp from which came the principal challenges to federal-ism is also fully documented.[19] By the time we come to the 1980s and the further moves towards integration, we are dealing of course with a younger generation, some of whom had already made their individual contributions. Even among the French there were suspicions of the degree to which decision-making was in the hands of the Brussels bureaucracy and it is Giscard d'Estaing who claims the credit for the invention of the European Council in 1978.

That innovation was intended to make the heads of the various governments directly responsible for the broad lines of policy which meant that until Maastricht the attempts to reach a common policy towards the rest of the world were excluded from the remit of the Commission, although the presidents of that body did manage to establish their right to a seat at the table.[20]

The political and hence military context of the development of the Communities tended to be underplayed in the discussions of the subject in many countries where the accent was on the alleged economic advantages. But this flight from reality was shown to be such as soon as the major international context changed as a result of two interconnected events – the collapse of the Soviet Union's hegemony in east and central Europe and the reunification of Germany. As we survey the scene in the mid-1990s and note the demographic and economic preponderance of Germany, we have to keep reminding ourselves that the logic of the Communities was Franco-German parity and that this has now disappeared. On the other hand some features of the earlier period remain. France is a nuclear power and Germany is not. France retains the possibility of projecting its military power outside the frontiers of the NATO states; Germany is inhibited by constitutional and still more by political considerations from doing so.[21]

With this perspective in mind we can see how specific were the circumstances in which France in 1950 embarked upon the project of a European Defence Community. Two points are essential for understanding its significance. In the first place, while the argument that this was the only way in which France and Germany could be prevented from going to war with each other will not hold water, it did involve a conscious decision in favour of a basically German alignment of French policy and in this sense the de Gaulle–Adenauer treaty, accompanied by de Gaulle's rejection of British membership of the EEC, was a continuation of this line of policy though from a very different ideological position.[22]

During the negotiations between 1950 and 1954 when the EDC project was rejected by France, it was clear that what was being proposed would not be acceptable to Britain which still had a global rather than a continental approach to the disposition of its military power. France also had overseas commitments which it tried to get its partners to take into account as the price of ratification. But when these were put to the other five governments at the Brussels Conference, the American ambassador actively intervened to make sure that the others did not give way. They did not and the treaty was rejected.[23]

The American intervention makes the second point clear. The attraction of the EDC was not simply that it presented a way of smoothing the path to German rearmament but that it was a step along the federal road. It would have been much simpler to adopt the solution that ultimately came about – the admission of Germany and Italy into what became the WEU and eventually into NATO. But that would not lead to the creation of a European Political Community as a step towards a federal Europe.

It is common among British students of these matters, as we have seen, to underplay the federalist aspect of the early moves towards European integration. It has even been argued that the new institutions created with American assistance amounted to a 'rescue of the Nation state'.[24] In fact the nation state did survive and its own institutions which had suffered during the war and under occupation were given new powers; but the impetus that had been given to federalism was only temporarily halted. In particular the French 'planners' from whom Monnet derived his economic techniques believed themselves to be serving a supranational not a national cause, as was true of their counterparts in the other countries of the Six.

The failure of the EDC saw Monnet quitting his post at the Coal and Steel Community and devoting himself to the building up of the European movement whose façade was provided by European politicians mainly of the Christian Democrat persuasion but which was, as already pointed out, dependent upon the injection of American funds.

It is worth noting that while in retrospect one can see the Treaty of Rome and the European Economic Community it created as providing through subsequent interpretation for big steps in the supranational direction, it was not so seen at the time by Monnet and the Euro-enthusiasts whose interests were not met by the idea of a 'Common Market', the name usually given to the EEC. It sounded too like the *laissez-faire* to which the enthusiasts for supranationalism were at heart opposed. The other product of the 1957 relaunch was Euratom which, had it produced a common policy for the future of atomic energy in Europe, would have had greater appeal. Such a common policy, given the military implications, was always unlikely; the French hoped that other countries might share the burden of developments in this field but this hope remained unfulfilled.[25]

Britain's absence from both these initiatives has been regarded as yet another instance of 'missing the bus'. In fact the situation was not dissimilar from that in 1950. The British were again asked to enter into negotiations whose outcome had been laid down in advance. The core of Europe had come to be the Franco-German partnership.

The subsequent development of policy in the European Communities was along lines favoured by the French, in particular the help given by the Common Agricultural Policy to the transfer of France's agricultural population into industrial and commercial employment, a rather belated experience of what other industrializing countries had already undergone. By the 1970s France's position was so secure that Pompidou could agree to the admission of the United Kingdom into the system and a decade later hail further moves towards integration – the Single European Act and the Treaty of Maastricht, including the commitment to a single currency which had been part of Monnet's original vision.

By then the domestic as well as the international background had altered. In the crucial period of the 1980s France had a socialist President and another French socialist was President of the European Commission, though, unlike most French socialists who were on the secular side in the basic ideological divide, Delors was a Catholic and could pursue his policies in comfortable partnerships with Christian Democrats in Germany, Italy and the Benelux countries. Christian Democracy was itself more at ease with the socialist parties of the continent since it also rejected the British Conservative dedication to *laissez-faire* and deregulation. British Conservatives who expressed sympathies with Christian Democracy were clearly unaware of this basic aspect of the European political scene, as was shown in the activities of the British Conservative members of the European Parliament who found it possible to group themselves with the European People's Party. The upholders of the British economic doctrines on the continent were the Liberal parties, and in France the major part of the Gaullist Right; but differences of nomenclature, themselves the product of history, afforded excuses for some odd alliances. The British Liberals of the David Steel–Paddy Ashdown variety had no readily visible continental counterparts.

During part of his presidency Mitterrand was obliged to 'cohabit' with governments of the Right. But the Constitution of the Fifth Republic designed by de Gaulle with a different political layout in mind meant that France's substantive position on European issues and in relation to Britain was mainly the product of Mitterrand's own instinctive preferences. It is too early to draw up a balance sheet of the Mitterrand era.[26] But some things about his outlook on the European issue can already be analysed to some effect.

It is not for nothing that Mitterrand reversed the normal stereotype of the French politician of the Third Republic which was to move from Left to Right. His own early commitment to the extreme Right in French politics has come in for much attention, particularly in his unwillingness to disclaim personal friendships with some of the regime's most suspect survivors.[27] But Vichy provides something of a clue to his international stance as well. Agreeing with de Gaulle that Britain was too closely linked to the United States and too interested in the wider world to be a truly European power, he confirmed the main choice made by the Vichy regime under Pierre Laval's leadership to accept German pre-eminence in Europe as inevitable and to make the best of it by becoming Germany's most loyal partner.

On the military side this meant forging a close association of part of France's armed forces with their German counterparts. But the alignment was not total, since the war in the former Yugoslavia for which clumsy and self-interested German diplomacy must take some of the blame saw France collaborate with Britain in giving armed support to the efforts of the United Nations and NATO.

On the economic side the commitment to the Maastricht goal of a single currency meant the alignment of the French franc upon the German mark requiring high interest rates with strongly deleterious effects upon the French economy, particularly as measures in terms of unemployment. Mitterrand acted upon the assumption that Germany's commitment to the single currency was absolute – as he might well have done given Chancellor Kohl's attitude – and seemingly attached no importance to the German Constitutional Court's ruling that the German Parliament had not surrendered its ultimate powers of decision. An approach taking into account the realities of German politics as they stood at the time Mitterrand left office might have concluded that what the Germans meant by a single currency was not something that would have involved putting its currency at the mercy of institutions in which weaker economies would have had a decisive voice, but simply the extension of the Deutschmark zone.[28] The Bundesbank would rule as before. How far French opinion was prepared to accept this end to the country's independence was far from clear when Mitterrand left office.

If one surveys the period during which Britain and France were both members of the Communities it is once again clear that their handling of membership was different. France went into negotiations with a clear idea of its minimum demands on the question at issue and a determination to secure compensation for any ground it had to give from its initial demands. The British tended if outvoted to retreat to their fall-back position without demanding anything in return. And the French were assisted, as Britain was not, by the fact that their own members of the Commission never overlooked the interests of France. France and Europe were to them as one.

With the election of the Gaullist Chirac as French President in 1995, it seemed possible that despite this identification of France and 'Europe' there might be room for closer Anglo-French cooperation since, as the Gulf and Bosnia had shown, there was a difference between two powers who could exercise military power 'out of area' and a still inhibited pacifist Germany. France, like Britain, was a permanent member of the UN Security Council because of the situation that existed when the UN was created. Both were now challenged as no longer deserving of such a role. Those who face a common challenge may come to find collaboration important. It was not for nothing that Britain stayed aloof from the protests against the French nuclear tests in 1995. While this was true of the German government, German opinion was less sensitive to France's needs. As EMU put the whole European enterprise into the melting-pot it was possible that the exclusive Franco-German partnership would come under question and French links with Britain receive some reinforcement.

7 Britain and the Crisis of European Union

Historians like finding turning-points. The turning-point in the history of the process of European Union set on foot by Jean Monnet and his collaborators had actually taken place a few months before the signature of the Treaty of Maastricht. The date was 20 June 1991 – the event the decision by the German Bundestag that the reunification of Germany (on 3 October 1990) should be followed by the resurrection of Berlin as the country's capital and the gradual move from Bonn to Berlin of the principal institutions of the federal government. As was seen in an earlier chapter, the basic inspiration of Monnet, Adenauer, Schuman and de Gasperi was the recreation of the Carolingian Empire. Berlin had not existed in Charlemagne's time and the region in which it was situated had never been part of that empire. It was then still contested ground between Teutons and Slavs.

The Germany of Adenauer had been able to take a distant view of the territories to the east of Germany since Soviet control seemed for the time being assured. There were more anxiety about the extension westwards of Soviet power than belief in the likelihood of its retreat. Germany which now saw things from the vantage-point of Berlin rather than Bonn and which faced at the same time both the collapse of the Soviet Empire and the emergence from under Soviet domination of some of the historic countries of central and eastern Europe would clearly have both different fears and different conceptions of where its national interest lay. Would its fears – of westward migration – or its hopes – of greater markets and openings for investment – be easily reconciled with the membership of an increasingly integrated European Union, some of whose members would have their own interests in the newly opened area.

131

More immediate was the impact upon the functioning of the European Union of the increase in the relative weight of Germany as against the other member states. After Britain's accession to the European Community in 1973, there had been a rough equilibrium in population between Germany, France, Italy and Britain, signalised by their allotment of two commissioners each and their quota of members in the European Parliament. That equilibrium no longer existed and on the latter point at least change was inevitable.

The most obvious way in which to handle the problem of the countries newly free to choose their own destinies was to extend the Union to the east as it had already been extended to the south. And 'enlargement' became a central feature of British policy at quite an early date. But, as the reunification of Germany had shown, to bring into the Union countries with a wholly different economic structure and a lower standard of living was bound to make demands on the existing members beside which their commitment to the poor 'south' would be relatively easy to handle. In particular it was hard to see how the Common Agricultural Policy could be applied to such new members. Nor was the half-way house of access to the markets of the Union itself such as served for the relatively wealthy Scandinavian potential members easily granted to countries whose lower labour costs might at any rate for a time make them dangerously competitive. Protectionism was still a force.

To tackle problems of this kind, as well as those with the rest of the world, developed and underdeveloped, for instance in relation to the General Agreement on Tariffs and Trade (GATT), the Union was ill-equipped and not rendered much better-equipped by the foreign policy 'pillar' of Maastricht.

While the Commission did provide the minimum degree of continuity which working out policies in these areas demanded, even a President with the energy of Jacques Delors could not apply the same degree of pressure as he had been able to exert on internal matters in the run-up to Maastricht. His successor would prove even less qualified for the task. What one had was a federal system with neither a President in the full sense nor a cabinet. The machinery for handling the decision-making progress in non-routine matters was left to the Presidents of the European Council for the time being and the presidency changed hands every six months. In the hands of major countries, this might work, though what was given priority might be too much affected by the national interests of the country concerned. For some of the small countries it was hard to provide from their slender administrative personnel even the minimum of work needed to keep the show on the road.

It would take some time for the full implications of the changes in the world scene to make themselves felt. What came first was the process by which the Maastricht Treaty came to be ratified, which, in its chequered course and not only in Britain, showed how far it was from the truth that the Maastricht compromises were solid ground. Without rehearsing the parliamentary history of the ratification in Britain which would take one into questions of internal party divergences on both sides, yet again, it is worth noting that it was the first occasion on which there was definite evidence of similar reactions to the movement of integration in a number of other countries. In many of them – as was to became clear over the next few years and in the run-up to the proposed revision conference scheduled in the treaty itself for 1996 – while there were a variety of provisions that caused questions to be asked, the common element was a feeling that the whole thing was something contrived by a narrow elite and somehow wished on the mass of the people who had hitherto not been consulted as to how far along the federalist path they really wished to go.

The Europhile elites had of course always acted internationally – the European movement in its various guises did attempt to influence public opinion in the different countries to accept a common programme. What was new was the coming together across national boundaries of the sceptics. For British political figures to be welcomed by the Danish 'no' campaign or for leaders of the French 'no' campaign to be listened to with interest and approbation in Britain was an unexpected and perhaps ironic commentary on the belief in a transnational European identity.

The chronology of the events shows how this came about. On 21 May, as we have seen, the House of Commons gave the Maastricht Treaty Bill a massive majority on second reading. On 2 June, the Danish people narrowly rejected the treaty in a referendum. The foreign ministers at a meeting on 4 June decided that the treaty provisions could not be renegotiated and that other countries should proceed with their own ratification procedures. The British government suspended consideration of the treaty in the hope that the Danes could be persuaded to reconsider their position. At the Lisbon Council meeting on 26–7 June, it was agreed that while patience with the Danes should be shown, renegotiation was ruled out. On 1 July, Britain took over the presidency for its six months' turn and would clearly have re-enlisting the Danes at the top of the agenda.[1]

The centre of attention was now France. It was necessary there to amend the constitution to cope with the treaty's provision for enfranchising European 'citizens' – a topic of particular importance in France because mayors are an important element in the electoral college for the Senate. French parliamentary opinion was in general still favourable to the Community and the revision went through with large majorities, culminating in the joint session of the Assembly and the Senate on 23 June. But the debates had revealed considerable differences within the parties of the Right, especially the Gaullist Ressemblement pour la République and Mitterrand had been tempted to cash in on them by calling for a referendum on 3 June. The referendum was fixed for 20 September and was seen by Mitterrand as a way of enhancing his authority after his recent and somewhat unrewarding attempts to take the lead in the remodelling of the new Europe.[2]

Once again, Mitterrand miscalculated. As so often in elections to the European Parliament, the voters were less concerned with the European issue posed to them than with the possibility of administering a snub to the government of the day; the unpopular socialist government of Pierre

Bérégovoy had little to commend it. Ratification was voted for by only 51.05 per cent of the electorate.

The French result helped to consolidate the anti-Maastricht feelings within the Conservative Party given voice to by Margaret Thatcher and former members of her cabinet. It was given a new twist by the desire in some quarters that the issue should be put to a referendum.[3] At the same time, the Labour Party was shifting towards a pro-Maastricht position consolidated when John Smith was elected leader in July 1982.

What had the most influence on Conservative opinion had occurred four days before the French referendum when, on 'black Wednesday', the pressure on the pound forced the chancellor, Norman Lamont, to end Britain's membership of the ERM. It was felt that the German unwillingness to revalue the mark or to lower interest rates was to blame for this débâcle although the subsequent recovery of the British economy which the freeing of its financial policy made possible was to alter the perception of the event, turning 'black Wednesday' into 'white Wednesday'. The event also provided arguments against Britain joining the single currency embodied in the Maastricht agreement.[4]

Major was more successful in pursuing an agreement which would enable the Danes to claim that there was sufficient reason for holding a second referendum, and the outlines of a solution were revealed at the Birmingham European summit in October. In November, the House of Commons returned to the Maastricht Treaty and a preliminary vote was held on November 4 at which the government carried the day by a mere three votes. It was now announced that the process would not be completed until after a second Danish referendum made possible in the Edinburgh Council in December when undertakings were given on 'subsidiarity', 'transparency' and 'openness'.[5]

The long-drawn-out process of ratification occupied Parliament for much of the first half of 1993. On 18 May the Danes in a second referendum approved the treaty by a comfortable majority, thus freeing the British government to go ahead.[6] It would be difficult to claim that the British debate added much to the understanding of the issues involved. While then and later there was much evidence of the harm done to particular British interests by Community legislation, it seemed impossible even for opponents of Maastricht on the Conservative side to grasp and make clear the fact that these consequences had at their root the single element of the sacrifice of national sovereignty to a federalist system to which the Maastricht Treaty was going to give a further impetus.

Indeed the running was made not by the Euro-sceptics within the Conservative Party but by the Labour Party seeking to reverse the opt-out from the social chapter. However the process was completed when the government made the issue one of confidence on 23 July and as far as Britain was concerned, Maastricht had been accepted. The only country whose ratification was needed to bring the treaty into effect was the main enthusiast for it, namely Germany. Amendments to the constitution were required to give effect to the new European citizenship, to allow the transfer of powers from the Bundesbank to the proposed European Central Bank and to safeguard the role of the *Länder* through the Bundesrat. How does one cope with the unit of a federal system which is itself a federation?

The Bundesrat seemed satisfied that the Länder could rely on the application of 'subsidiarity'. But the Bundestag, perhaps echoing the known worries of the Bundesbank about the sacrifice of the mark for a new European currency, attached to its ratification resolution (which was passed by 543 votes to 17 on 2 December 1992) an amendment insisting on the fulfilment of the convergence criteria for EMU before it could come into effect. The government also accepted the Bundestag's demand for a positive vote of assent before stage 3 of EMU – the single currency – could come into effect. In a sense this was to say that Germany, while claiming to be an enthusiastic partisan of EMU, had achieved much the same kind of opt-out mechanism as Major had obtained for Britain at Maastricht.

A further hold-up was created by a case brought before the German Constitutional Court seeking to prevent the

President's signing the treaty on the ground that it still violated the Basic Law despite the new amendments to the latter. In finding against the appellants, the Court delivered a long and complicated interpretation of the treaty. The court denied that the Union had been given any general area of competence and maintained that the new specific powers conferred upon the institutions were limited to what was required to fulfil the objectives of the treaty. As has been noted earlier, the Court defined the Union as a Staatenverbund, thereby denying it the character of a state. It also insisted that German participation must depend upon the Union obtaining and retaining a degree of democratic legitimacy for its actions. Democracy must be embodied in the Union's own institutions and in those of the member states. On the basis of this analysis, commentators of a federalist inclination have argued that 'the growth of European federal democracy is a constitutional imperative for Germany'.[7]

With this last obstacle out of the way, the German President could sign the treaty which entered into effect on 1 November 1993.[8] But by this date the atmosphere of consensus which appeared to have existed at Edinburgh had clearly disappeared. On the one hand, the federalist drive on the part of the Commission continued with the implementation of the second Delors 'package' for extra expenditure by the Commission.[9] On 26 August the new French Prime Minister, Edouard Balladur, who had taken office after the Socialists' defeat in the French general election in March, met with Chancellor Kohl at Bonn and confirmed the commitment of the two countries to European integration, despite the fact that earlier that month, the ERM had virtually collapsed, leading Major to assert that the Maastricht timetable for EMU had become unrealistic.

And as evidence mounted of the continued Franco-German commitments to press on with the European enterprise, British opinion, particularly inside the government and the Conservative Party, seemed to be moving in the opposite direction. It was becoming clear that the mere rejection of the social chapter would not prevent the use of other provisions in the Treaty of Rome itself to impose further regulation on the British economy. But mindful no doubt of the still unfinished business of British ratification, when the Labour ministers adopted by a qualified majority the 48-hour week on 2 June 1993, Britain was guaranteed a ten-year renewable exemption.

It was clear that both party sentiment and perhaps a gradual hardening of his own convictions meant that Major himself regarded Maastricht as a limit to the process of integration except in so far as it seemed worthwhile leaving open participation in the single currency. But while there could on many issues be delays until the 1996 Intergovernmental Conference, there were problems created by enlargement which needed to be faced. One was the question of the distribution of votes in the European Council with its consequences for the blocking minority which could be used in the event of it proceeding to voting by qualified majority. Major made an unsuccessful fight to retain the existing situation but found himself obliged to accept an unpalatable compromise.[10]

In 1993–4, the government was losing ground as the result of various difficulties on the domestic side leading to an electoral débâcle in the local government elections of May 1994. These took place while the elections for the European Parliament were also in progress. Once again it seemed likely, as proved to be the case, that the voters in Britain as elsewhere would act in accordance with their general political sentiments of the moment rather than on European issues which nowhere aroused great interest – either in Britain or on the continent. But the growing impatience of the Euro-sceptics in the British Conservative Party made it difficult to fight a convincing campaign when many of its candidates for the European Parliament were on the party's other wing. The European People's Party added to these difficulties by drafting a strongly federalist manifesto, including the social chapter, though it was stated that their associates, the British Conservative MEPs, were not bound by it. How MEPs could act in opposition to the grouping of which they formed part was not clear. In the event such refinements passed the electorate by and the result of the election was a pronounced fall in the Conservative representation and, as has been noted, a more significant rise in Labour's presence in the Parliament.

The surviving Conservative MEPs were to provide with some exceptions a continued irritant to the party as a whole, tending to treat themselves as the voice of Brussels at Westminster rather than the reverse, as was shown in the course of the Party Conference in October 1995.

In a sense the arguments at the time of the Euro-elections and after were a continuation of the previous divergences over European integration, particularly in the economic and social fields. There were also anxieties about the effect of French protectionism on the long-drawn-out negotiations for the Uruguay round of the GATT although in the end a fairly satisfactory conclusion was reached.

On the provisions respecting foreign policy and defence, the third pillar of Maastricht, there were deeper anxieties. Major's first challenge as Prime Minister had been the Gulf War in which British armed forces played an important part alongside and under overall control of their American allies. But there was little evidence of solidarity on the part of Britain's European 'partners'. The Belgians – the great apostles of integration – refused even to sell the ammunition required by the British forces. It could be added that both at this time and subsequently, while Britain and the United States tended to see eye to eye on the problems of the whole region and in particular respecting the equally nauseating regimes in power in Iran and Iraq, some European countries, including France and Germany, seemed to be governed by narrower commercial considerations.

Far more serious was the effect upon the embryonic European Union of the break-up of Yugoslavia.[11] Although western Europe shared a common interest in preventing the break-up resulting, in the internecine war between its constituent ethnic groups that actually happened and perhaps in a wider Balkan conflict, the way in which this desire was interpreted was clearly felt differently in each of the major countries. It provided another occasion of showing how feeble was the method of leaving initiatives to the presidency of the European Council at the time and how little of a reinforcement was given by the 'troika', the President's association with his immediate predecessor and immediate successor. It also showed that the new enlarged Germany now had a foreign policy of its own and was prepared within its constitutional limitations to forward it in every possible way.

From the autumn of 1992 the impact of these and other external events, as well as the growing concern about Europe's falling competitiveness and its common problems of unemployment and the financing of the welfare state, produced in the United Kingdom on the one hand and in the continental members of the European Union on the other quite different responses, each consistent with its own assumptions but hard to reconcile with each other. The elaboration of these rival visions of Europe ran into a variety of obstacles. While there were domestic problems in a number of the continental countries leading to some questioning of the validity of the assumptions upon which the federalist vision was based, the difficulties arose primarily from the different expectations of the various states and their governments. In Britain the difficulties were largely internal and largely confined to the governing Conservative Party. Since no decisions would need to be taken until the Intergovernmental Conference of 1996 and in the case of the single currency even later, the general tendency of the other governments and of the Commission was not to confront the divergences directly but to go on reiterating the hope that, perhaps after a change of government, Britain would clamber aboard the common craft. Similarly on the British side, the Prime Minister and the foreign secretary (until July 1995) Douglas Hurd continued to express the belief that Britain's alternative vision would in the end find general favour.[12]

The divisions in the Conservative Party followed along the lines that had developed during the debates on the ratification of the Maastricht Treaty. It was not so much that the

Euro-sceptics could not assent to the essentials of the Prime Minister's position as set out in his celebrated article in *The Economist* in September 1992, as that they doubted his ability to persuade the other countries of its wisdom and felt that he was neglecting the very different trends that were taking shape in the discussions elsewhere of the Union's future, and the continued activity of the Community's institutions in directions considered by them inimical to Britain's interests.

By the beginning of 1995 the divergences had gone so far and the unease in the party was so profound that active rebellion was seen as no longer out of the question. The occasion came with the need for a bill to make possible meeting the higher demands for payment into the Community's funds.[13] The rebels were deprived of the party whip which meant that the government was now without a majority of its own. And this in turn produced so much discussion of a possible challenge to the Prime Minister in the autumn that he decided that his position would be totally weakened unless he could bring the issue forward and in the wake of the electoral disasters in the 1995 local elections challenge his opponents head-on by resigning the party leadership and standing for reelection. His opponent proved to be not a 'stalking horse' but a member of his own cabinet, John Redwood, the Secretary of State for Wales. Mr Major's majority in the ballot was sufficient to make it plain that the party had no option but to stay with him until the next election. The rebels were readmitted to the whip and the cabinet reshuffled.

The reshuffle of July 1995 was of some importance from the point of view of the presentation of Britain's position in the run-up to the Intergovernmental Conference (IGC).[14] Hurd was replaced at the FCO by Malcolm Rifkind, not known as an out-and-out Euro-sceptic but, as he was to show in his speech at the Party Conference in October, certainly more overtly sympathetic to their fears. His successor as Secretary of State for Defence, Michael Portillo, was a known Euro-sceptic and not disposed to conceal his own doubts about some interpretations of the common defence aspect of pillar 3 of Maastricht. These questionings revived the debate across national boundaries and the President of the Commission, Jacques Santer, and the senior British commissioner, Sir Leon Brittan, gave public expression to their disapproval of the line taken by the two British ministers. The hopes of the Europhile wing of the party rested more than ever on the chancellor of the exchequer, Kenneth Clarke, who refused the Euro-sceptic demand to rule out for the foreseeable future any thought of Britain taking part in the single currency.

It is evident that the government was conscious of the fact that while the European Union provided the most important individual market for British exports and that this helped to explain the gratifyingly high degree of inward investment from the United States, Japan and South Korea, it did not overlook the fact that much of Britain's business was engaged in countries far distant from the European Union, and that global trends seemed to suggest that this might prove the most important element of growth. Of course other major countries in the Union were following their own agendas in respect of overseas trade and its stimulation, but London felt itself to be the centre of a worldwide network of trade and investment to a greater extent than any other European capital.

A similar perception of global interests rather than interests confined to the continent of Europe explained the difficulties that the UK found in carrying forward the Maastricht ideas about a common foreign and defence policy. While it was desirable that Britain should find itself aligned with other friendly countries in major issues of foreign policy, neither in the Middle East nor in the Balkans had such an alignment within the European Union proved possible. Furthermore all British governments since 1945 had made it their first priority not to separate themselves from the United States. Britain was unlikely to agree to any arrangements by which it might be obliged in deference to a European vote to risk coming into collision with the United States.

Such a perspective was even more telling in respect of defence. British forces had been used to operating within the context of an alliance. They had shown in Bosnia that they could act effectively in conjunction with the French. It was not pretended that the country could afford forces that could enable Britain to act on its own in a major campaign, but the focus of any cooperative effort remained NATO. The idea that a military arm of equal value could be created out of the WEU and then embodied within the European Union to the extent of developing a single European army was something which no British government was likely to countenance. If other countries wanted to go down that path, they would have to do so without the United Kingdom.

One must not assume that it was only Britain which had particular foreign policy concerns and objectives. A significant difference was also emerging between those countries in the north and particularly Germany who thought that assistance to central and eastern Europe with a view to the eastward enlargement of the Union should be the focus of effort, and France, Italy and Spain who wanted help to be given to the Maghreb (not extending to importing its products) for obvious domestic reasons.

A further source of British concern was the role of the European Court.[15] While it was the case that the flow of European legislation in the form of directives and regulations was actually slowing down, the interpretations placed upon existing directives and even upon the actual clauses of the Treaty of Rome produced uncertainty about the state of the law. The habit of the Court of giving retrospective effect to its interpretations had also meant in some cases the imposition of vast and unquantifiable financial obligations upon the governments of member states. Harmonisation beyond what was needed to make the Common Market effective still seemed to inspire the Court's activities. And although Britain had during the Maastricht negotiation supported the idea of imposing penalties upon states in breach of their obligations, the actual levying of very large fines, as had taken place, was hardly reconcilable with the idea of national sovereignty to which the British government was publicly committed.

Various ideas for remedying this state of affairs were apparently being mooted in the run-up to the IGC – limiting the Court's powers to make its judgments retrospective, curtailing the powers of lower national courts to seek its views, and providing for the publication of dissenting judgments by the Court itself. No doubt these and other measures if they found general favour would meet some of the complaints of citizens and businesses as well as governments. One cannot say to what extent. The difficulty is that it is almost impossible to see how any substantial changes could be made without revising the Treaty of Rome itself. Everything the Court did was in its view compatible with the treaty provisions to which it owed its existence. The situation was the same as in the case of the Common Agricultural Policy, reform of which was dear not only to the British government but even to the Euro-enthusiasts of the official Opposition. It was in the treaty.

It seemed certain that when the IGC did meet, Britain would find that once in a federal system, one cannot pick and choose between its component elements, particularly when they are at the heart of the original conception. There was no indication that a revision of the Treaty of Rome was on the IGC agenda.

It is clear that if this is a correct summary of the essentials of the British position as it stood in the autumn of 1995, it could only lead to a negative approach to the Intergovernmental Conference, and such reports as were made available of the preparatory work being done for that conference indicated that the British role was being perceived in that light. It is perhaps not surprising that the body of Conservative members of the House of Commons favourable to further Europe integration styled themselves the 'positive Europe group'.

What was equally obvious was that what on the continent was professedly the majority current of opinion was a totally different version of the future goal. To some extent this was concealed by the use of such phrases as a 'two-speed' or 'multi-speed' Europe, for this suggested that the exponents of the traditional Monnet version of Europe simply wished to go faster than the British – the same goals reached at different speeds. The truth was that they wanted something quite different – it was not merely the speed but the goal that was the subject of abiding controversy. What was unacceptable to the Commission, the German CDU, the majority in the European Parliament and their allies in the Low Countries, Italy and Spain was the idea, often given voice to in Britain, of a Europe of 'variable geometry', that is to say, a series of arrangements between different groups of countries for common action in the areas where they found this appropriate.

What the upholders of the Monnet version wanted was what they had wanted from the beginning – a fully federal organisation of Europe in which, subject to temporary derogations, all member states would participate. In practical terms it meant not risking further enlargement until the central institutions had been given greater powers – 'deepening' before 'widening' as the phrase went. It meant regarding the Maastricht device of the three 'pillars' as a mere expedient to bring Britain and Denmark along. The ultimate purpose should be to bring all the Union's activities within the purview of the Commission, the Court and the Parliament, to insist upon total freedom of movement within the Union, and the subordination of national citizenship to the European citizenship created by the treaty. In that case there could be a single European army whose use would be governed by the normal decision-making procedures of the Union. Of such a more perfect union, the single currency would be at once the symbol and the guarantee.[16]

The tactics for bringing about this objective included threats of commercial sanctions. Of course, it was asserted, national identity would be preserved even when the nation state had been transformed into a unit in the federation with no scope for individual action in the economic, environmental or social fields except as such action under the 'subsidiarity principle' might be delegated to the local legislatures or administrations. It was not admitted that part of a nation's identity might be embodied in its own inherited political and judicial institutions just as much as in its language and literature and artistic heritage.

It is possible to speak of the crisis of the Union in 1995 because of two interlocking features of the European scene. In the first place the continuation in a period of economic recovery of high levels of unemployment and the social tensions that this created meant that enthusiasm for the whole enterprise was harder to summon up except among groups who could see some direct benefits to themselves from their country's membership. The French and the Spaniards were beginning to see that struggling to achieve the Maastricht criteria which involved the subordination of their currencies to the Deutschmark was not productive of any favourable consequences as far as the majority of the population was concerned.[17] It was generally believed that a country like Sweden which had so recently accepted the obligations of membership was now so disillusioned that a further referendum would probably come to the opposite conclusion. In the second place it was increasingly clear that not all the thirteen countries which had not claimed an opt-out would in fact be qualified under the Maastricht criteria to join the single currency by 1999. And quite apart from the fear of Chancellor Kohl in particular that the opportunity might be lost if his guiding hand was removed, there seemed no reason to believe that a mere postponement by a couple of years or so would make a vital difference.

By 1995 realism had crept into the discussions to the extent that it was openly admitted that the adoption of the single currency would be confined to a limited number of states – that there would be an inner group within the wider community. While the British and Danish opt-outs at Maastricht might be said to have paved the way for such an outcome, it was far from the original concept of the Union. Only a very limited number of small countries would clearly meet the Maastricht criteria by the due date – if they alone were to go along with Germany, what would have happened would be a mere extension of the Deutschmark zone. To give any serious significance to the move, at least one other major economy must be embodied in the system – and that would have to be France. As late as 25 October 1995 after a bilateral meeting Chancellor Kohl and President Chirac publicly expressed their confidence that the two countries would go ahead together in 1999.

Such assertions could not be taken at their face value. Even more serious than French worries about the economic effects of EMU was the evidence that now that the Germans were for the first time being told that they were to give up their monetary sovereignty, they found the prospect unappealing. Could the prudent Germans be expected to finance the looming deficits not only of France but of Spain and Italy as well? Yet so deeply committed was the German elite to the notion of European Union that this could not openly be stated. What was being mooted instead as the crisis deepened was the idea that the Maastricht criteria were too weak; countries might be obliged under Maastricht to meet specific criteria of financial rectitude at the date of entry into EMU but what if they then relaxed into profligacy? Was it not necessary to give some central authority powers to intervene not only in their monetary affairs but in their fiscal systems?

From the German point of view such provisions would be logical. But if it was admitted that such powers would need to be vested in the new European monetary authority, it made nonsense of all the claims by Kenneth Clarke and others that EMU did not of necessity imply political union. The Euro-sceptics had won the argument; former Europhiles like Douglas Hurd were beginning to suggest that it was time not to push further on the international road but to pause, take breath and see where one had got to.

The crisis of European union was not of Britain's making, nor could Britain produce a solution. What was really happening in the summer and autumn of 1995 was the discovery in continental Europe that the whole European federal idea had been the preserve of a small but powerful elite which had never thought it necessary to take the general public into its confidence. Now it was becoming a matter of genuine debate in Germany as it had been in France since the time of Mitterrand's referendum. And what came out did not accord with what Chancellor Kohl was telling his foreign counterparts, still less with what the increasingly vocal and increasingly remote European Parliament was proclaiming. Some kind of European system there would have to be, but it looked increasingly unlikely that it would be a Europe in the Carolingian mode.

Unlikely but not impossible. On the eve of a visit by President Chirac to John Major, the French MEP Elizabeth Guigou to whose views we have had occasion to refer more than once, said on the BBC (*Today* programme, 27 October 1995) that France would have to choose between the German vision for Europe and the British vision; they could not be reconciled. The same old dilemma again, how would France choose and what would Britain do?

Notes and References

1 The Problem Stated

1. See Alain Peyrefitte, *L'Empire immobile ou le choc des mondes* (Paris, 1989), translated by Jon Rothschild as *The Collision of Two Civilizations* (London, 1993).
2. See on this aspect of the problem the two books by Richard Pipes, *The Russian Revolution 1899–1919* (New York and London, 1990) and *Russia under the Bolshevik Regime, 1919–1924* (New York and London, 1994). The rather abundant literature on 'fellow-travelling' in the later period of the Soviet Union's history has to be revised in the light of the increasing flow of new information on that period.
3. The fact that this should be so justifies the attempt to classify Hitler and Stalin together, as in Alan Bullock, *Hitler and Stalin, Parallel Lives* (London, 1991).
4. The basic argument will be found in my pamphlet, *A Tale of Two Europes*, published in May 1993 by the (London-based) Institute for European Defence and Strategic Studies.
5. For the background to de Gaulle's action, see Charles Williams, *The Last Great Frenchman: A Life of General de Gaulle* (London, 1993) pp. 408ff.
6. An insight into the world of the Commission can be derived from Roy Jenkins, *European Diary, 1977–1981* (London, 1989). But since that time, the pretensions of the Commission have notably advanced, particularly under the presidency of Jacques Delors from 1985 to January 1995. See Charles Grant, *Delors: Inside the House that Jacques Built* (London: Brealy, 1994).

2 The Historical Perspective

1. Jeremy Black, *Convergence or Divergence? Britain and the Continent* (London, 1994).
2. For an analysis of how a British notion of nationhood came about in the early modern period, see Linda Colley, *Britons: Forging the Nation 1707–1837* (London, 1992).
3. Philip Williams, *Hugh Gaitskell, a Political Biography* (London, 1979), p. 729.
4. On Churchill's position see Chapter 4.
5. For English translations of these documents see A. R. Myers (ed.), *English Historical Documents* (ed. David C. Douglas) Vol. IV, pp. 656 and 659–62.

6. Ibid., p. 484.
7. See on this point Alan Macfarlane, *The Origins of English Individualism* (Oxford, 1978).
8. On the latter argument see Jonathan Clark, *English Society, 1688–1832* (Cambridge, 1985).
9. See Paul W. Schroeder, *The Transformation of European Politics, 1763–1848* (Oxford, 1994).
10. No Conservative opponent of joining the Communities on economic grounds has left a full account of these transactions, but the position of a Labour free-trader is well depicted in the memoirs of Lord Jay: Douglas Jay, *Change and Fortune: A Political Record* (London, 1980).
11. A. V. Dicey, *Introduction to the Study of the Law of the Constitution*, was first published in 1885. Many later editions have maintained its classic status.
12. Lord Hailsham, *On The Constitution* (London, 1992) ch. XVI, 'Sovereignty: The European Dimension'.
13. M. Pinto-Duschinsky, *The Times*, 17 August 1994.
14. Lord Jay seems to have been the only public figure for whom accepting the continental vision of a United Europe was the equivalent of the 'appeasement' of Hitler in his drive to continental domination Jay, *Time and Chance*, p. 357). But some echoes of that feeling can be found in some of Lady Thatcher's utterances.
15. For this aspect of the matter, see Max Beloff, *Imperial Sunset*, Vol. 2, *Dream of Commonwealth* (London, 1989).
16. For the wartime relationships of the three powers, see Robin Edmonds, *The Big Three: Churchill, Roosevelt and Stalin in Peace and War* (New York and London, 1991). On Truman's handling of the situation which he inherited from Roosevelt, see David McCullough, *Truman* (London, 1992).
17. For one view of this aspect of the matter, see Max Beloff, 'The end of the British Empire and the assumption of world-wide commitments by the United States', in W. R. Louis and Hedley Bull (eds), *The 'Special Relationship'* (Oxford, 1986).
18. Max Beloff, *The United States and the Unity of Europe* (Washington, DC 1963) p. 103.
19. Max Beloff, *The United States and the Unity of Europe* (Washington, DC: The Brookings Institution, 1963) p. 103. How US policy had developed to this point from a very different wartime position is described in the earlier chapters of that work.
20. Acheson's own memoirs, *Present at the Creation: My Years in the State Department* (New York, 1969), gives an important account of that crucial phase in postwar history.
21. Quoted in Douglas Brinkley, *Dean Acheson, The Cold War Years, 1953–71* (New Haven, Conn. and London: Yale University Press, 1992) p. 176.
22. For Monnet's own view of his role in history see Jean Monnet, *Memoirs*, trans. Richard Mayne (London, 1978).

23. Brinkley, *Dean Acheson*, 187–9.
24. Ibid., pp. 176ff.
25. The reply took the form of a letter to Lord Chandos who had sent Macmillan a protest on behalf of the Institute of Directors which was made available for publication in the British press: Harold Macmillan, *At the End of the Day* (London, 1973) pp. 339–40.
26. Henry Kissinger, *Diplomacy* (New York & London: Simon & Schuster, 1994) pp. 547–8.
27. Ibid., p. 577.
28. Ibid., p. 592.
29. Ibid., p. 548.
30. Ibid., p. 597.
31. Ibid., p. 618. For a challenging account of Anglo-American relations in the twentieth century, see Donald Cameron Watt, *Succeeding John Bull: America in Britain's Place, 1900–1975* (Cambridge, 1984).
32. An account of the progress of the federal idea in the interwar years and during and immediately after the war will be found in Max Beloff, *Europe and the Europeans: An International Discussion*, a report prepared at the request of the Council of Europe (London, 1957).
33. Coudenhove-Kalergi and other figures of second-order political rank continued to put forward various ideas for European union. Their influence in Britain is much overrated by Andrea Bosco in his book *Federal Union and the Origins of the 'Churchill Proposal': The Federalist Debate in the United Kingdom From Munich to the Fall of France* (London: Lothian Foundation Press, 1992). The 'federalist debate' had very little to do with Churchill's last-minute plea to the French in June 1940. Lord Lothian was the principal British figure to entertain such notions. See John Turner (ed.), *The Larger Idea: Lord Lothian and the Problem of National Sovereignty* (London, 1988).

3 Federalism and Federalists

1. For Jean Monnet and his legacy see the narrative of his career by one of his acolytes, François Duchêne, *Jean Monnet: The First Statesman of Independence* (New York and London, 1994). In describing the differences over the future of Europe that emerged in the early period of the Consultative Assembly of the Council of Europe, Paul-Henri Spaak, a devoted admirer of Monnet, calls those in favour of greater measures of integration 'federalists'. The word was perfectly acceptable to those of that way of thinking: P.-H. Spaak, *Combats inachevés*, Vol. 2 (Paris, 1969) pp. 30–3.

2. Ernest Wistrich, *The United States of Europe* (London, 1994) p. 2. Mr Wistrich was President of the Commission for European Citizenship of the European Community.

3. A dedicated pro-European has argued that Eden's agreement not to remove British forces from Europe without the agreement of a majority of members of the new WEU was an agreement based on 'supranationalism': Spaak, *Combats inachevés*, Vol. 2, pp. 310–11.

4. A former MEP Lady Rawlings, argued as late as June 1995 that the British saw federalism as something centralising while the Germans saw it as a form of decentralisation. That is to confuse two different things. Compared with a wholly centralised government like that of France or the UK, a federation does give some power to regions and is therefore decentralising. But for an independent country to enter a federation is to accept rule from a 'centre' where none has previously existed. House of Lords, Paper 88, session 1994–5.

5. The French who had little experience of federalism were still fully aware of what the word meant. For instance the prewar Socialist Party used the word 'federations' to describe its organisation in each department since these federated their separate local branches.

6. For a description of the German system, see William E. Paterson and David Southern, *Governing Germany* (Oxford: Blackwell, 1991). For the text of the Constitution (Basic Law) see S.E. Finer, V. Bogdanor and B. Rudden, *Comparing Constitutions* (Oxford, 1995).

7. See Timothy Garton Ash, *In Europe's Name: Germany and the Divided Continent* (London, 1993). In a lecture at Chatham House on 19 January 1995, Dr Kurt Biedenkopf, the prime minister of Saxony, emphasised the need to make more of the federal aspects of the German Constitution suggesting in particular that the spending of European funds should be delegated the regional authorities, the Länder. He also pointed out that the European Parliament could not act in legislative matters or in the control of the Executive as did national parliaments. The work of the Bundesrat was intergovernmental.

8. For this early phase of Britain's involvement with Europe, see Max Beloff, *Europe and the Europeans*, a report prepared at the request of the Council of Europe (London: 1957).

9. See, e.g., Lord McCluskey, *Law, Justice and Democracy* (London, 1986) pp. 45ff.

10. The treatment here of the development of the legal and constitutional aspects of the Communities is based upon three studies by legal luminaries: Lord Mackenzie Stuart, *The European Communities and the Rule of Law* (London, 1977); Gordon Slynn, *Introducing a European Legal Order* (London, 1992) and the paper by Sir Patrick Neill, QC, presented as evidence to the House of Lords Select Committee on the European Communities as part of their consideration of the problems facing the Intergovernmental Conference scheduled for 1996: Session 1994–5, Select Committee, 18th Report,

Minutes of Evidence, HL Paper 88, July 1995 pp. 218ff. Lord Mackenzie Stuart and Lord Slynn both served as judges on the European Court of Justice and are 'Europhile' by inclination.

11. R. David and J. E. C. Brierley, *Major Legal Systems in the World Today*, 3rd edn (London, 1985) pp. 22–3. For European Law see Stephen Weatherill and Paul Beaumont, *EC Law* (London, 1993).

12. Mackenzie Stuart, *The European Communities*, pp. 50–4. Since that was written there has of course been a considerable expansion of judicial review in Britain.

13. Not many judges have the robust good sense of a London magistrate who was confronted with a Belgian motorist who had refused to be breathalysed because European law prevented self-incrimination. 'I am afraid Strasbourg at the moment doesn't overpower me and you are guilty by British law.' £300 fine, £250 costs, 11 months driving ban. *The Times*, 22 December 1994.

14. Jean-Claude Casanova: 'Es gibt kein logische Unterscheidung zwischen dem Prinzip der Subsidiariat und dem des Federalismus. Entweder bleiben die Staaten souverän, oder sie geben ihre Souver-"anitat" schrittweise ab.' *Die Verfassung Europas*. Bergdorfer Geschprahkreis Protokoll, No. 103, Korber Stiftung, Hamburg, 1995. p. 20.

15. Charles Grant, *Delors: Inside the House that Jacques Built* (London, 1994) p. 218.

16. *Die Verfassung Europas*, p. 9.

17. It is customary to give particular praise to the House of Lords Select Committee on the European Communities and its reports are indeed a major source of information on every aspect of the Communities' functioning. It is not often noted that the actual debates to which they give rise or other debates dealing with European issues are less satisfactory since they tend to be dominated by ex-commissioners whose devotion to their former incarnation is usually boundless. There were seven of them in the House in 1995 as well as several former MEPs. One must add that, as will be seen in Chapter 7, one of the ex-commissioners, Lord Tugendhat, expressed some misgivings at the acceleration of federalist moves in the post-Maastricht period.

18. On the foundations of American constitutional thinking see Alexander Hamilton, James Madison and John Jay, *The Federalist*, ed. Max Beloff, 2nd ed (Oxford: Basil Blackwell, 1987).

19. House of Lords Select Committee on the European Communities, Session 1994–5, 18th Report, HL Paper 88, p. 219. What follows is largely drawn from Sir Patrick Neill's written evidence. The claim by Lord Mackenzie Stuart that it is a travesty of the Court's powers and duties to say that it can 'overturn statutes, reinterpret directives and invent and impose new laws' (Letter in *The Times*, 26 August 1995) will hardly bear examination. The Court has constantly reshaped the legal systems of member countries in quite detailed ways and in pursuit of its own aspirations towards a 'new legal order', as set out

in Lord Mackenzie Stuart's own book published eighteen years earlier.

20. Since the procedures of the Court require that all judgments be unanimous with no dissenting opinions made public, it is of course hard to know what impact the arguments of individual judges may have had. This makes the jurisprudence of the ECJ much more opaque than that of the US Supreme Court.
21. Weatherill and Beaumont, *EC Law*, pp. 317–22.
22. Ibid., pp. 323–5.
23. Ibid., pp. 325–6.
24. Ibid., pp. 322–3.
25. HL Paper 88, pp. 251–2.
26. Weatherill and Beaumont, *EC Law*, pp. 180–2.
27. See George Ross, *Jacques Delors and European Integration* (Oxford, 1995).
28. *The Sunday Times*, 1 October 1995.

4 Europe in British Politics, 1945–75

1. See Max Beloff, 'The Anglo-French Union Project of 1940', reprinted from *Mélanges Pierre Renouvin* (Paris, 1966) in Max Beloff, *The Intellectual in Politics* (London, 1970).
2. See Max Beloff, 'Churchill and Europe,' in Robert Blake and Wm. Roger Louis (eds), *Churchill* (Oxford, 1993).
3. 'The United Nations Plan for Organizing Peace' FO Paper, 7 July 1943, printed in Sir Llewellyn Woodward, *British Foreign Policy in the Second World War*, Vol. V (London, 1976).
4. Stuart Croft, *The End of Superpower: British Foreign Office Conceptions of a Changing World, 1945–1951* (Aldershot, 1994) p. 45.
5. Ibid., p. 78. For the French approach see Chapter 6 of this volume.
6. On the defence aspects of British thinking at this time, see Julian Lewis, *British Military Planning for Post-war Strategic Defence, 1942–47* (London, 1988).
7. Croft, *The End of Superpower*, pp. 114–18.
8. Kenneth O. Morgan, *Labour in Power, 1945–1951* (Oxford, 1984) pp. 274–5.
9. For the negotiations of these treaties see the detailed account in Alan Bullock, *Ernest Bevin, Foreign Secretary 1945–51* (London, 1983) pp. 513–684.
10. It has been argued that Bevin's rather vague language about Western European Union made the continentals and particularly the French

believe that Britain would be prepared for much more binding constitutional ties with western Europe since they were accustomed to think in forms of written constitutions and found British projections of a gradualist approach too vague. See John W. Young, *Britain, France and the Unity of Europe, 1945–1951* (Leicester: Leicester University Press, 1984) pp. 104–17, 185–91.

11. Beloff, 'Churchill and Europe', pp. 448–9.
12. Bullock, *Ernest Bevin*, pp. 622–3.
13. On the Council of Europe and its work in relation to other European institutions, see Max Beloff, *Europe and the Europeans* (London, 1957).
14. Bullock, *Ernest Bevin*, pp. 778ff.
15. On the US reaction see Max Beloff, *The United States and the Unity of Europe* (Washington, DC, 1963) ch. V.
16. Croft, *The End of Superpower*, pp. 162ff.
17. Beloff, 'Churchill and Europe', pp. 452–3.
18. For Eden's attitude to European issues, see Robert Rhodes James, *Anthony Eden* (London, 1986), and Richard Lamb, *The Failure of the Eden Government* (London, 1987).
19. See Alan Milward, *The European Rescue of the Nation-State* (London: Routledge, 1992) pp. 81–197.
20. Peter Lyon, 'The Commonwealth and the Suez Crisis' in Wm Roger Louis and Roger Owen (eds) *Suez 1956: The Crisis and its Consequences* (Oxford, 1989) p. 272.
21. Eric Roll, *Crowded Hours* (London, 1985) p. 99.
22. Richard Lamb, *The Macmillan Years, 1957–1963: The Emerging Truth* (London, 1995) pp. 102–3. This work is the first to be written on the period since the opening of the public records for those years and despite the author's strong pro-European bias is an important guide to the negotiations of the time.
23. Max Beloff, 'The Crisis and its Consequences for the British Conservative Party', in Wm. Roger Louis and Roger Owen (eds), *Suez 1956*, p. 334. It could be added that Prime Minister Menzies of Australia's strong support for Britain was to be the last echo of the solidarity of the pre-1939 'Old Commonwealth'. New Zealand held aloof and Canada followed the United States line, its policy being strongly tinged with 'Third World' and United Nations sentiment. See the chapters by J. D. B. Miller and Michael G. Fry in Louis and Owen (eds), *Suez 1956*.
24. See Maurice Vaisse, 'Post-Suez France', in Louis and Owen (eds), *Suez 1956*.
25. See Harold Macmillan, *Riding the Storm 1956–1959* (London, 1971) ch. III. Alistair Horne, *Macmillan*, Vol. 1.2 (London, 1989) pp. 31–3.
26. For the text of 'Plan G' see Macmillan *Riding the Storm* (London, 1971) pp. 753–4.
27. For Macmillan's own account of the moves towards a changed policy, see Harold Macmillan, *Pointing the Way 1959–1961* (London,

1972) ch. 3, 'Sixes and Sevens'. In his biographer's view, Macmillan believed that EFTA was only 'a stopgap on the road to unity': Horne, *Macmillan*, Vol. II, *1957–1986*, p. 217.

28. John Campbell, *Edward Heath: A Biography* (London, 1993) pp. 112–13.
29. Ibid., pp. 48–9, 74–5.
30. It was something strongly pressed for by the foreign secretary, Selwyn Lloyd; there is no evidence that he was particularly a supporter of European integration. See D. R. Thorpe, *Selwyn Lloyd* (London, 1989), p. 297.
31. HC Deb., 12 February 1959. For Maudling's view of these negotiations see Reginald Maudling, *Memoirs* (London, 1978) pp. 67–75, 232–3.
32. See Anthony Howard, *RAB: The Life of R.A. Butler* (London, 1987) pp. 295–6. For his conversion to a pro-market position, see Horne, *Macmillan*, Vol. II, p. 353.
33. Lamb, *The Macmillan Years*, p. 137.
34. CAB 129/102. I am indebted to Professor Peter Hennessy for communicating this document.
35. Horne, *Macmillan*, vol. II, pp. 109–13, 128–9.
36. Ibid., pp. 256–7.
37. A pioneer attempt to set the whole story of Britain's attempts to enter the EEC in the light of party alignments at home was made by Uwe Kitzinger in his book, *Diplomacy and Persuasion: How Britain joined the Common Market* (London: Thames & Hudson, 1973). Although much new material has emerged since then and although the author is a dedicated 'European', there is much in this volume that would be hard to find elsewhere.
38. Horne, *Macmillan*, Vol. II, pp. 354–5.
39. For Macmillan's own account, see Harold Macmillan, *At the End of the Day* (London, 1973) chs I, V and XI. For a much revised version, see Lamb, *The Macmillan Years*, ch. 9.
40. Horne, *Macmillan*, Vol. II. p. 314.
41. Ibid., pp. 306–7.
42. Ibid., p. 328.
43. For de Gaulle's attitude to Britain at this time, see Charles Williams, *The Last Great Frenchman* (London, 1993) pp. 431ff.
44. Lamb, *The Macmillan Years*, pp. 147–8.
45. Ibid., p. 156.
46. Philip M. Williams, *Hugh Gaitskell: A Political Biography* (London, 1979).
47. I have followed the account in Williams, *Hugh Gaitskell*, ch. 25. In her biography of Tony Crosland, published after Philip Williams's book appeared, Susan Crosland treats the whole question of EEC membership in terms of the Left–Right balance within the party, and the ambitions for the leadership of Roy Jenkins. See Susan Crosland, *Tony Crosland* (London, 1982).
48. Williams, *Hugh Gaitskell*, p. 710.
49. Ibid., p. 708, See also Roy Jenkins *A Life at the Centre* (London, 1991) p. 145; Douglas Jay, *Change and Fortune* (London, 1980) p. 282.

50. Williams, *Hugh Gaitskell*, p. 712.
51. Ibid., p. 729.
52. Ibid., pp. 733–6.
53. John Murray, 'The Dream that Turned to Ashes', *The European Journal*, April 1995.
54. See Ben Pimlott, *Harold Wilson* (London, 1992) p. 579.
55. On receiving the news of de Gaulle's veto, Heath speaking in Brussels had affirmed Britain's determination not to turn its back on Europe. Campbell, *Edward Heath*, p. 131. When Wilson submitted to the House of Commons the government's decision to renew Britain's application, it was approved by 488 votes to 62. The Opposition included only 21 socialists alongside 21 Conservatives, 6 Ulster Unionists and the one Welsh Nationalist.
56. Jay, *Change and Fortune*, pp. 347ff.
57. R. H. S. Crossman, *Diaries of a Cabinet Minister*, Vol. 2 (London, 1976) pp. 30–7.
58. Ibid., pp. 81ff; 101, 104, 113, 116.
59. Ibid., p. 303.
60. Ibid., pp. 320–1.
61. Jay, *Change and Fortune*, p. 424.
62. Ibid., p. 428. Gordon-Walker, whose interests had been mainly in Commonwealth matters, was to hold other offices and became a strong pro-EEC supporter. See Patrick Gordon-Walker, *Political Diaries, 1932–1971* (London, 1991).
63. Susan Crosland, *Tony Crosland*, p. 336.
64. David Owen (Lord Owen), *Time to Declare* (London, 1991) p. 248.
65. Crossman, *Diaries*, Vol. II pp. 333 ff.
66. Ibid., p. 336.
67. Gordon-Walker, *Political Diaries*, pp. 312–13.
68. Crossman, *Diaries*, Vol. II, pp. 406, 505, 695.
69. Campbell, *Edward Heath*, pp. 352–9.
70. Margaret Thatcher, *The Path To Power* (London: HarperCollins, 1995), p. 232.
71. Campbell, *Edward Heath*, pp. 396–405.
72. Gordon-Walker, *Political Diaries*, pp. 326–8.
73. For Tony Benn's shift see Jack Adams, *Tony Benn* (London, 1992) pp. 330–1.
74. Campbell, *Edward Heath*, pp. 437–41.
75. HC Deb., 13 June 1972. Howe's own account of his role in these proceedings and the manner in which he reconciled himself to the notion that parliamentary sovereignty and membership of the EEC could be combined is in Geoffrey Howe, *Conflict of Loyalty* (London, 1994) pp. 65–9.
76. Campbell *Edward Heath*, p. 557.
77. Ibid., p. 607.
78. For Harold Lever's role, see the obituary 'Lord Lever of Manchester' in *The Times*, 7 August 1995.

79. Edmund Dell, *A Hard Pounding: Politics and Economic Crisis, 1974–6* (Oxford, 1991) p. 16.
80. On Wilson's handling of the issue, see Pimlott, *Harold Wilson*, pp. 575–611.
81. Dell, *A Hard Pounding*, p. 17.
82. Barbara Castle, *Diaries, 1974–1976* (London, 1986) pp. 128–9.
83. Ibid., p. 212.
84. James Callaghan, *Time and Chance* (London, 1987) pp. 300 ff.
85. Jenkins, *A Life at the Centre*, p. 387.
86. Austen Morgan, *Harold Wilson* (London, 1992). pp. 456–7.
87. Communiqué of Council of Ministers, Paris, 9–10 December 1974, Cmnd. 5830.
88. Tony Benn, *Against the Tide, Diaries 1973–6* (London, 1989),p. 285.
89. Castle, *Diaries, 1974–1976*, p. 287.
90. Jay, *Change and Fortune*, pp. 481–4.
91. Benn, *Against the Tide*, pp. 342 ff. Benn himself made the prescient point that the Common Market was a threat to the unity of the United Kingdom: 'there will be no valid argument against an independent Scotland with its own Ministers and Commissioners enjoying Common Market membership'. By the 1990s this was a staple argument of the SNP.
92. Jenkins, *A Life at the Centre*, pp. 399 ff.
93. Campbell, *Edward Heath*, pp. 683 ff.
94. Thatcher, *Path to Power*, pp. 331–5.
95. Callaghan, *Time and Chance*, p. 325.
96. Castle, *Diaries*, p. 390; Jay, *Change and Fortune*, pp. 483–90. Basing himself on the subsequently published official figures, Lord Jay estimates the balance in financial terms as ten to one.
97. Max Beloff, 'European Hamiltonians', *The National Interest*, no. 40, Summer 1995.
98. Jay, *Change and Fortune*, p. 487.
99. Campbell, *Edward Heath*, p. 686.
100. Sir Roger Tomkys in *Parliamentary Brief*, February 1995, p. 33.
101. Lord Aldington in House of Lords Select Committee on the European Communities, *1996 Intergovernmental Conference*, Minutes of Evidence, H. L. Paper 88, Session 1994–5.

5 Europe in British Politics, 1975–91

1. Denis Greenhill (Lord Greenhill), *More by Accident* (York, 1995).
2. Nicholas Henderson, *Mandarin: Diaries of an Ambassador* (London, 1994) 24 March 1974, p. 59.

3. Ibid., 1 October 1978, p. 214.
4. Ibid., 5 October 1978, p. 218 For an account of the negotiations of the EMS by the then British President of the European Commission, see Roy Jenkins, *Life at the Centre* (London, 1991) ch. 26.
5. Henderson, *Mandarin*, 29 January 1979, p. 248. For the issue of the British position in respect of the Community budget see Jenkins, *Life at the Centre*, ch. 27.
6. Barbara Castle, *Diaries 1974–6*, 12 February and 26 March 1976, pp. 650 and 705–6.
7. Given the pro-EEC stance of the Labour government at the time of the referendum in 1975, continental socialists must have been rather taken aback by the swiftness of the party's about-turn. In 1980 the Labour Party's annual conference voted for unconditional withdrawal from the Community and in the election of 1983 campaigned for this step to be taken. Barbara Castle herself was an MEP from 1979 to 1989, and was part of the party's later shift towards a pro-European stance.
8. For the rise and fall of the SDP and the 'Alliance' with the Liberals, see Jenkins, *Life at the Centre*, pp. 474–534. It is interesting to note the nomenclature since on the continent 'Social Democrats' were part of the Marxist tradition in socialism, however far from that some the parties may have travelled in the 1950s and 1960s. It is yet one more example of how different and incompatible are the positions of the parties in the different European countries.
9. The problem for the British parties in this general context is well-illuminated in David Butler and Martin Westlake, *British Politics and European Elections, 1994* (London, 1995).
10. For an account of the monetary aspect of the Community's aims and achievements from a distinctly Europhile point of view, see John Pinder, *European Community: The Building of a Union* (London, 1991) ch. 7, 'Monetary System and Monetary Union'.
11. For Lady Thatcher's own account of her premiership, see Margaret Thatcher, *The Downing Street Years* (London, 1993).
12. See Charles Grant, *Delors: Inside the House that Jacques Built* (London, 1994).
13. For the interaction between German national goals and the European enterprise, see Timothy Garton Ash, *In Europe's Name, Germany and the Divided Continent* (London, 1993).
14. See George Ross, *Jacques Delors and European Integration* (Oxford, 1995), for an examination of the economic background.
15. Fortunately we have accounts of these events from both the chancellor and the foreign secretary. See Nigel Lawson, *The View from No. 11* (London, 1992); Geoffrey Howe, *Conflict of Loyalty* (London, 1994). See also Margaret Thatcher, *The Downing Street Years*, (London 1993).
16. According to his biographer it took until a speech in the House of Commons on 26 July 1990 for Heath to refer openly to Britain as a unit in a federal system: John Campbell, *Edward Heath*, p. 800.

17. See the article by Lord Buxton, 'Euromania has become a cult', *Contemporary Review*, October 1995.

18. 'The Single European Act contrary to my intentions and my understanding of the formal undertakings given at the time had provided new scope for the European Commission and the European Court to press forward in the direction of centralization' (Margaret Thatcher, *The Path to Power* (London, 1995) p. 473).

19. Howe, *Conflict of Loyalty*, pp. 397–403.

20. Ibid., pp. 305–8.

21. Thatcher, *The Downing Street Years*, p. 314.

22. Lord Cockfield, *The European Union: Creating the Single Market* (London, 1994) p. 141.

23. For a brief account of these transactions see John Pinder, *European Community: The Building of a Union* (London, 1991) pp. 60ff.

24. Thatcher, *The Downing Street Years*, p. 547.

25. Cockfield, *The European Union*, pp. 150–1.

26. Thatcher, *The Downing Street Years*, pp. 548–59.

27. Grant, *Delors*, pp. 65–73.

28. Howe, *Conflict of Loyalty*, pp. 457–8.

29. Thatcher, *The Downing Street Years*, p. 556.

30. Santer was to emulate Delors by addressing the British TUC at its annual conference. The idea of some kind of non-political executive hardly fits in with appealing to a particular interest group in a member country to oppose its own government's policies.

31. Thatcher, *The Downing Street Years*, pp. 588–9.

32. See Grant, *Delors*, ch. 7, 'The Push for a Federal Europe'.

33. Lawson, *The View from No. 11*, ch. 71.

34. Ibid., p. 907. (Paris, 1969)

35. Paul-Henri Spaak, *Combats inachevés* Vol. 2, p. 67.

36. Lawson, *The View from No. 11*, p. 907.

37. Butler and Westlake, *British Politics*, pp. 22–32.

38. Bernard Connolly, *The Rotten Heart of Europe*, (London, 1995) pp. 104–6, makes the case for a Delors conspiracy.

39. Howe, *Conflict of Loyalty*, pp. 643 ff.

40. Thatcher, *The Downing Street Years*, p. 833.

41. Text in Howe, *Conflict of Loyalty*, appendix II.

42. This aspect of the Delors approach is made abundantly and convincingly clear in George Ross, *Jacques Delors and European Integration*.

43. Kenneth Baker, *The Turbulent Years* (London, 1993) pp. 348 ff.

44. Ibid., p. 351. While this would make it appear that Kenneth Baker was strongly pro-Community, by the time of the Conservative Party Conference in 1993 he had moved into a distinctly Euro-sceptic position.

45. For a useful analysis of the Maastricht Treaty, albeit written by Europhiliacs, see A. Duff, J. Pinder and R. Pryce, *Maastricht and Beyond: Building the European Union* (London, 1994).

46. See Rodney Atkinson and Norris McWhirter, *Treason at Maastricht: The Destruction of the Nation State*, 2nd edn (London, 1995) chs 4 and 5.

47. It might be appropriate to call attention to the dedication to this topic of the journalist Christopher Booker whose weekly contribution to the *Sunday Telegraph* listing the more bizarre and damaging pieces of Community legislation and cases of their enforcement by zealous officialdom has helped to keep the subject alive.

6 Britain, France and European Union

1. The book *Building Post-War Europe: National Decision-Makers and European Institutions, 1948–1963*, edited by Anne Deighton (London: St Martin's Press, 1995), deals with the Italian, Belgian and Dutch contributions to the process as well as the roles of France, Britain and Germany.
2. See Max Beloff, 'The Anglo-French Union Project of 1940', in *The Intellectual in Politics* (London, 1970).
3. See François Duchêne, *Jean Monnet* (London, 1994); Charles Grant, *Delors: Inside the House that Jacques Built* (London, 1994); and the review under the title 'European Hamiltonians' by Max Beloff in *The National Interest*, no. 40, Summer 1995. See also George Ross, *Jacques Delors and European Integration* (Oxford, 1995).
4. See Elizabeth Guigou, *Pour les Européens* (Paris, 1994). Madame Guigou was one of the two MEPs appointed to the 'Reflection Group' set up to prepare for the 1996 Inter-governmental Conference.
5. A recent work has thrown much light on the role of the Church during the Vichy regime: W. D. Halls, *Politics, Society and Christianity in Vichy France* (Oxford: Berg, 1995).
6. Vincent Auriol, *Mon septennat, 1947–1954*, eds P. Nora and J. Ozouf, abridged edn (Paris, 1970) p. 380.
7. Benjamin Disraeli, *Letters*, Vol. 5 (Toronto, 1993) p. 456 n.
8. See Alan Milward, *The European Rescue of the Nation State* (London: Routledge, 1992) pp. 219ff.
9. See Richard Lamb, *The Macmillan Years 1957–1963: The Emerging Truth* (London, 1995) pp. 192ff.
10. I am indebted to Professor David Dilks for letting me have his two unpublished lectures 'Rights, Wrongs and Rivalries: Britain and France in 1945' and 'De Gaulle and the British'. The general course of the negotiations is summarised in John W. Young, *Britain, France and the Unity of Europe, 1945–1951* (Leicester, 1984).
11. See Claude d'Abzac Epezy and Philippe Vial, 'In Search of a European Consciousness: French Military Elites and the Idea of Europe, 1947–1954', and Gerard Bossuat, 'The French Administrative Elite and the Unification of Western Europe, 1947–1958', in Anne Deighton (ed.), *Building Postwar Europe*.

12. René Massigli, *Une comédie des erreurs, 1943–1956* (Paris, 1978).
13. The diaries of Vincent Auriol provide a running commentary on these issues from the point of view of the traditional Left. See Auriol, *Mon septennat*, and also Jean Lacouture, *Pierre Mendés-France* (Paris, 1981).
14. See on this point, R. O. Paxton and Nicholas Wahl (eds), *De Gaulle and the United States* (Oxford: Berg, 1994) on de Gaulle's attempt to secure a Three-Power directorate. See Paul-Henri Spaak, *Combats inachevés*, Vol. 2, pp. 180–7.
15. See Max Beloff, *The United States and the Unity of Europe* (Washington, DC, 1963), and 'European Hamiltonians', *The National Interest*, no. 40, Summer 1995.
16. The British clearly needed to know what the balance within the Community was likely to be; in answer to Macmillan's inquiry in 1960 he was informed as follows: 'The French will have the greatest influence in the next few years and may be able to retain it. But much will depend on the future of France after de Gaulle's departure and upon developments in Germany. The Germans particularly if there was a swing to the Right backed by industrialists might well make a determined challenge for the leadership' (CAB 129/102, 1960).
17. Massigli, *Une canédie des erreurs*, p. 195. The degree to which the Americans were a driving force behind the movement towards a 'United Europe' and of Monnet's dependence upon US funds has been shown in a convincing fashion in two articles by Richard J. Aldrich, 'European Integration: An American Intelligence Connection', in Deighton (ed.), *Building Postwar Europe*, and 'OSS, CIA and European Unity: The American Committee on United Europe, 1948–1960', (unpublished).
18. See Robert Marjolin, *Architect of European Unity, Memoirs 1911–1986*, trans. William Hall (London, 1989); Etienne Hirsch, *Ainsi va la vie* (Lausanne, 1988); Hervé Alphand, *L'Etonnement dêtre: Journal 1939–1975* (Paris, 1978); Pierr Uri, *Penser pour l'action* (Paris, 1991); and Raymond Poidevin, *Robert Schuman, homme d'état, 1886–1963* (Paris, 1986)).
19. See Jean Lacouture, *De Gaulle*, 3 vols (Paris, 1984, 1985, 1986); Michel Debré, *Trois Républiques pour une France, Mémoires*, 3 vols (Paris 1985–1988); and Maurice Couve de Murville, *Le Monde en face* (Paris, 1989).
20. Valéry Giscard d'Estaing, *Le Pouvoir et la vie* (Paris, 1988) pp. 119–21.
21. For a very penetrating examination of Germany's dilemma over the use of military force and the anxieties its new status has created for the French see Franz-Josef Meiers, 'Germany: The Reluctant Power' *Survival*, vol. 37, no. 3, Autumn 1995.
22. For the Franco-German treaty of 22 January and de Gaulle's disappointment when it was watered down by the German Parliament in order to preserve the special nature of Germany's relation-

ship with the United States, see Charles Williams, *The Last Great Frenchman: A Life of General de Gaulle* (London, 1993) pp. 432ff.
23. Debré, *Mémoires*, Vol. II, p. 221.
24. See Milward, *The European Rescue of the Nation-State* (London, 1992).
25. The French attached reservations to their signature of the Euratom treaty to prevent it interfering with their military aspiration. Spaak, *Cambats inacherés*, Vol. 2, pp. 188–202.
26. An interesting first attempt is that of John Laughland, *The Death of Politics: France under Mitterrand* (London, 1994). Revealing of Mitterrand's methods are the diaries of Jacques Attali, Jacques Attali, *Verbatim*, Vol. 1 (Paris, 1994).
27. See Pierre Péan, *Une jeunesse française, François Mitterrand, 1934–1947* (Paris, 1994).
28. The choice of waiting for the convergence of the economies before monetary union was one the French made in the negotiations for Maastricht. The Germans would have been prepared to go ahead with the countries that qualified. See Christiane Saint-Etienne, *L'Europe contre le Capitalism* (Paris, 1993).

7 Britain and the Crisis of European Union

1. Apart from Denmark, the smaller countries were unlikely to put up obstacles. Ireland, the great financial beneficiary, voted to ratify by a large majority in a national referendum and Greece by an even more decisive parliamentary vote did the same.
2. On Mitterrand's failure to get to grips with what was happening either in the former Soviet Union or in central and eastern Europe, see John Laughland, *The Death of Politics: France under Mitterrand* (London, 1994), pp. 247 ff.
3. As one of the 176 peers who voted for a referendum amendment, I should put it on record that I saw this as a last-ditch attempt to secure the bill's defeat. I do not believe myself that in a parliamentary democracy the referendum is an appropriate method for deciding great national issues. If a referendum had been called and the treaty approved I would not have felt bound to suspend opposition to a surrender of sovereignty which no single generation has the right to make. In the event no such decision was called for since no fewer than 445 peers went into the government lobby. The list of those who voted for a referendum the *sanior* though not the *major pars* will be found in Atkinson and McWhirter, *Treason at Maastricht: The Destruction of the Nation State*, 2nd edn (London, 1995), pp. 146–8.

4. The role of the Bundesbank in trying to establish a dictatorship over all European exchange rates and interest rates is explored in Bernard Connolly, *The Rotten Heart of Europe.* (London, 1995).

5. The French used the Edinburgh summit to extort an agreement that sessions of the European Parliament would continue to be held at Strasbourg. The division of the Community's work between Brussels, Luxembourg and Strasbourg has been one of the main factors in its extravagance and inefficiency.

6. It should be pointed out that Danish objections to the treaty were quite different from the British ones. Britain wished to prevent the Union from imposing extra controls in the industrial, social and environmental spheres; the Danes were fearful that their own high standards might be diluted and their non-participation in defence matters challenged. Norway, which was to reject EU membership, was a member of NATO. Denmark, which remained in the EU, was not.

7. A. Duff, J. Pinder and R. Pryce, *Maastricht and Beyond: Building the European Union* (London, 1994) p. 62.

8. A challenge in the British High Court by Lord Rees-Mogg to the validity of the ratification process in the UK was dismissed on 30 July.

9. George Ross, *Jacques Delors and European Integration* (Oxford, 1995), p. 196.

10. David Butler and Martin Westlake, *British Politics and European Elections, 1994* (London, 1995) pp. 54–62.

11. For an early and penetrating analysis of the international implications of the break-up of Yugoslavia, see John Zametica, *The Yugoslav Conflict* (Adelphi paper), No. 270 (London: IISS 1992).

12. The most elaborate exposition of Mr Major's position was in a lecture delivered at Leiden University in the Netherlands on 7 September 1994; what we want be said is a Europe 'which does not impose undue conformity but encourages flexibility . . . a Europe which is free and secure, prosperous and coherent, democratic, potent and generous'.

13. An increase in the ceiling of the Community's so-called 'own resources' from 1.2 per cent to 1.21 per cent of GNP was agreed by the European Council on 31 October 1994. The European Communities (Finance) Bill passed the House of Commons in December.

14. In a letter to all chairmen of Conservative Associations on 20 July 1995 after his re-election as party leader, Mr Major outlined among other aims his intentions with respect to Europe: 'I believe in a free market, free trading Europe, built upon nation states. A wider Europe, spreading the benefits of peace and prosperity far to the East'.

15. The Court itself, so far from being willing to see any curtailment of its activities, was ambitious to extend them particularly in relation to pillars 2 and 3 of the Maastricht Treaty from which it had been

excluded. See the European Court of Justice, 'Report of the Court of Justice on Certain Aspects of the Treaty on European Union', 24 May 1995, summarised by David Pannick, QC, in *The Times*, 16 August 1995.

16. Jacques Santer, who took readily to the role of a propagandist for further integration, proclaimed the 'benefits' of European union in a speech at the Guildhall on 4 May 1995, and in a speech to the TUC on 11 September 1995 dismissed all talk of the possibility of the single currency resulting in job losses.

17. While opposition to Maastricht had been largely guided in France by elements of the Right, there were also left-wing opponents, including in particular the former minister Jean-Pierre Chevènement. He reacted unfavourably to the suggestions from the German Christian Democrats for the further transformation of the political aspects of the European Union: 'l'idé de transformer la Commission de Bruxelles en gouvernement responsable devant le Parlement européen, et le conseil Européen en seconde Chambre' ne peut que susciter en France un formidableé éclat de rire. Cette idée manifeste hélas, la profondeur du fossé culturel qui separe encore l'Allemagne et la France' (*Le Monde*, 12 October 1994).

Index